teach
them
diligently

How to
Use the
Scriptures
in Child
Training

Lou Priolo

TIMELESS TEXTS
Woodruff, SC

To Gabriella

The Lord [is] my strength and song,
And He has become my salvation;
He [is] my God, and I will praise Him;
My father's God, and I will exalt Him.
Exodus 15:2

I pray that you will grow *strong* in the Lord
and in the power of His might, *strong* in
spirit, filled with wisdom (for a wise man is
strong), and *strong* in the grace that is in
Christ Jesus.

Acknowledgments

In addition to Dr. Jay Adams, whose previous book *How to Help People Change* has laid the groundwork for this volume, I'd like to thank the following individuals for their helpful contributions:

Jay Younts—who was the first to teach me the application of 2 Timothy 3:15-17 to biblical parenting and who graciously gave me permission to publish much of his material in this book.

Fern Gregory—who has in countless ways helped me with this project.

Dr. Wayne Mack—who has taught me much in the way of using the Scriptures to diagnose and correct life's problems.

Dr. Den Trumbull—for his help with Chapter Six.

Capt. Scotty Anderson—for his assistance with Appendices A and F.

Brenda Payne—for her insights into how to make this book more user friendly to women, and for her assistance with Appendix E.

Kimberly Priolo—for her encouragement and willingness to sacrifice a little of her husband's time so that he could minister to others through the writing of this book.

The Session of Eastwood Presbyterian Church—who in a variety of ways have enabled me to complete this book so quickly.

Preface

So many books... so little Scripture

The bookshelves in your home no doubt contain volumes of books, manuals, seminar notes, magazine articles, and video and audio cassettes purporting to address parenting from a Christian point of view. Some of these works, while claiming to be biblical, may actually contain "insights" that were gleaned from humanistic pop-psychology but are foreign to the Bible. Other tools in your parenting tool chest are doubtless very biblical and helpful. With rare exception, however, most of today's Christian parenting resources fail[1] to emphasize what is perhaps the most important aspect of true biblical parenting—*how to relate the Bible to the disciplinary process in practical ways.* Think about it. With all of your training, do you *really* know how to use the Bible for *doctrine, reproof, correction, and instruction in righteousness* with your children? If you do, you probably will not need to read any further. If you don't, it is my prayer that this little book will augment and strengthen your parenting skills as you learn how to use the Scriptures more thoroughly and effectively in your child training.

Lou Priolo

---

[1] I am aware of at least one Christian parenting "expert" who has repackaged his child training material with most of the Scripture removed in an attempt to reach a secular market. If you removed the Scripture from a truly Christian parenting model, it would (and should) fall as flat as a pancake. It is *the Scriptures* that we are to teach diligently to our children in the milieu of everyday living.

Author's Note

Don't do it!

As you begin this book, you may soon become overwhelmed by the sheer amount of information to which you will be exposed. At times you may feel like you are taking a drink from a fire hydrant and are drowning in the process. You may even find yourself asking, "How am I ever going to be able to do all that?" Don't be discouraged, and, whatever you do, don't stop reading. The "good stuff," the practical advice, the material which will give you the most hope and encouragement is more toward the back of the book.

Don't expect to be able to utilize all that you learn overnight. Change takes time. You must be patient with your children, yourself, and especially with your spouse in the process of implementing this material.

You may also become quite convicted of your own "want of conformity unto or transgression of the Law of God" as it pertains to your parenting duties and priorities. Admittedly, this book is very convicting—even to its author. But parenting in general, and teaching your children the Bible in particular, are by far two of the most important and time-consuming responsibilities God has given you. So, should the Holy Spirit convict you of anything, confess your sin to God, and then commit to developing a course of action that will gradually facilitate a more biblical approach to using the Scriptures in your child training.

Contents

...from childhood you have known the sacred writings which are able to give you the wisdom that leads to salvation through faith which is in Christ Jesus. All Scripture is inspired by God and profitable for teaching, for reproof, for correction, for training in righteousness.

2 Timothy 3:15-16

chapter one
The Scriptures and Your Children

Have you ever stopped to ask yourself what it is you are trying to accomplish as a parent? What exactly is your objective? Since you are a Christian parent there is only one ultimate answer to this question—and that answer is found in the Bible. The supreme objective you should have for your children is the same objective the Apostle Paul had for his spiritual children—that they be conformed to (gradually changed into) the image of Christ.

> My children, with whom I am again in labor until Christ is formed in you… (Gal. 4:19)

The Bible describes this "Christ-likeness" in a variety of ways. Terms such as "perfect" or "complete," "sanctification," and "the measure of the stature which belongs to the fullness of Christ" (to name a few) are employed by Paul (and other New Testament authors) to communicate a heartfelt desire to see those under his spiritual care attain the goal of Christian *maturity*.

> And we proclaim Him, admonishing every man and teaching every man with all wisdom, that we may present every man complete in Christ. (Col. 1:28)

> Until we all attain to the unity of the faith, and of the knowledge of the Son of God, to a *mature man*, to the measure of the stature which belongs to the fullness of Christ. As a result, we are *no longer to be children*, tossed here and there by waves, and carried about by every wind of doctrine, by the trickery of men, by craftiness in deceitful scheming; but speaking the truth in love, *we are to grow up* in all [aspects] into Him, who is the head, [even] Christ. (Eph. 4:13-15, emphases added)

1

How wonderful! Your objective (that which you are attempting to accomplish) as a parent has already been laid out for you in the Bible. You don't have to wonder what your child should become. You know what your child is supposed to look like when you're finished training him. He is to look like Jesus Christ.

The Key Ingredients

There are at least three essential ingredients necessary to produce the Christ-like maturity you are to be endeavoring to produce in your children. They are the *Spirit*, the *Scriptures,* and *time*. *First* it is necessary for a person to be changed into the image of Christ by the Holy Spirit. This gradual transformation takes place on the inside of a person—in his heart. The Holy Spirit indwells only those individuals who have, by God's grace, trusted in the atoning work of Christ Who died on the cross (as a substitute) for (to pay the penalty for) their sins (Rom. 5:8; 1 Cor. 15:3; 2 Cor. 5:21). You, too, must depend on God's Spirit to help you become the kind of parent the Bible requires of you.

The *second* maturity-producing resource is the Bible. Now the interesting thing to note is that the Scriptures are necessary to help your child realize the basics of salvation, such as his sinful condition and his need to trust in Christ's substitutionary death on the cross. You see, no one can become a Christian without the Bible (cf. Rom. 10:13-17). The Spirit works through the Word to bring conviction and ultimately regeneration (1 Peter 1:23). Because the Scriptures are able (have the power) to make your children wise about salvation, it is essential that you begin using the Scriptures with your children at an early age.

> ...and that from *childhood* you have known the sacred writings which are able to give you the wisdom that *leads to salvation through faith* which is in Christ Jesus.
> (2 Tim. 3:15, emphasis added)

Charles Spurgeon, in his book *Come Ye Children: A Book for Parents and Teachers on the Christian Training of Children,* addresses the term "from a child."

The expression, "from a child," might be better understood if we read it, "from a very child;" or, as the Revised Version has it, "from a babe." It does not mean a well-grown child, or youth, but a child just rising out of infancy. From a very child Timothy had known the sacred writings. This expression is, no doubt, used to show that we cannot begin too early to imbue the minds of our children with Scriptural knowledge. Babes receive impressions long before we are aware of the fact. During the first months of a child's life it learns more than we imagine. It soon learns the love of its mother, and its own dependence; and if the mother be wise, it learns the meaning of obedience and the necessity of yielding its will to a higher will. This may be the key-note of its whole future life. If it learn obedience and submission early, it may save a thousand tears from the child's eyes, and as many from the mother's heart. A special vantage-ground is lost when even babyhood is left uncultured.

The Holy Scriptures may be learned by children as soon as they are capable of understanding anything.[1]

Just in case you're wondering whether or not little children really can learn the Scriptures, allow me to recount for you a couple of episodes from personal experience.

I was lying on my bed one afternoon waiting for my wife to finish dressing when she asked me to bring her something she needed. Sophia, our (then) two-year-old daughter, was standing between us as I sighed grudgingly in response to Kim's request for my assistance. Immediately my little girl, who of course couldn't yet read, said ever so sweetly, "Daddy, you should '*Do all things without complaining or arguing.*'"

Several weeks later (days after her third birthday) the three of us were in a restaurant waiting for our food. The waitress had just

---

[1] Charles Spurgeon, *Come Ye Children: A Book for Parents and Teachers on the Christian Training of Children* (available on CD-ROM from Ages Software, 1-800-279-4307), p. 66.

brought a coloring place mat and some crayons for Sophia to entertain herself with while our food was being prepared. I was seated across the booth from the girls watching my little artist desecrate the place mat with her scribblings and scrawlings. At this point I went into teacher mode. The wise counselor (who should have known that a three-year-old is not developmentally able to do so) began trying to teach his daughter how to color *inside the lines*. I picked up a crayon and, beginning at the top of the paper, proceeded to color as neatly as I could upside down. Little by little I encroached my way down the sheet until my large paw was crowding out her petite hand. Picture this: my forearm is resting across the entire length of the place mat, my hand is at its bottom and Sophia has no place to color. At that moment she looked up and said "Daddy, the Bible says, '*Do not forget to do good and to share.*'"

Not only did my daughter know the Scriptures at a young age, but she was able to effectively minister them to her college educated father. If my two-year-old daughter can benefit from learning the Scriptures, so can your children.

Since the bulk of this book has to do with the practical use of the Bible, please permit me to ask you a few tough questions about the extent to which you minister the Word to your children.

- How well do you know the Scriptures yourself?
- How often do you refer to the Bible in the course of normal conversation with your children?
- How adept are you at *teaching* and relating the Scriptures to them in everyday life?
- How effectively do you use the Scriptures to *reprove* (convict) them of their sin? (Do you reprove in such a way that causes them to revere God's Word or to disdain it?)
- How consistently do you use the Bible when you *correct* them?
- How do you use the Bible to *train* your children in *righteousness* to help them to do better in the future?

You see, it's simply not possible to bring up your children "in the discipline and instruction of the Lord" (Eph. 6:4) without the continuous use of God's Word. It is "the rod *and reproof*" that "give wisdom" (Prov. 29:15). It is your job, Christian parent, to both *know and use* the Scriptures as God intended.

The Sufficiency of Scripture

The Scriptures provide all you need for life and godliness (2 Peter 1:3). They also provide all you need to bring up your children "in the discipline and instruction of the Lord." For thousands of years[1] Christian parents have depended on the Bible as their source for child training. Down through the centuries men and women have believed that God would not ask them to do anything without giving them the resources to accomplish the task—especially a task as difficult as raising godly children. They believed it when Paul told them that the Scriptures were given "in order to make the man from God adequate, and to equip him fully for every good task" (2 Tim. 3:17, CCNT).

Do *you* believe that? I mean, do you really believe God has given you within the pages of your Bible resources adequate for dealing with every contingency you face both in life and as a parent? That's really what this verse teaches. Of course, the Bible doesn't purport to be adequate for dealing with medical problems, teaching your children how to multiply fractions, roller skate, hit a baseball, and suchlike, but it does claim to be sufficient when it comes to changing people into the image of Jesus Christ. "The law of the Lord is perfect, restoring the soul" (Ps. 19:7).

The Fourfold Use of the Scriptures

When the Bible speaks of the Scriptures being profitable, it means that they are *useful*. "All Scripture [is] given by inspiration of God, and [is] *profitable* [*lit.* useful] for *doctrine*, for *reproof*, for *correction*, for *instruction* in *righteousness*" (2 Tim. 3:16, NKJV). Since the Scriptures have been given for these distinct purposes, you must become proficient in all four of these applications. The process of biblical child training involves using all four of these distinct activities. You see, biblical parenting is not only a responsibility, it's also a skill that must be

---

[1] For over 19 centuries the Church of Jesus Christ did not have the "benefit" of clinical psychology to assist them with parenting. Yet for centuries, Christian parents were still able to obey God's command to "bring up" their children "in the discipline and instruction of the Lord" (Eph. 6:4).

developed. This brings us to the *third* resource necessary to produce Christian maturity in your child—time.

It takes time to develop parenting skills. It takes time to drop whatever you may be doing and pick up your Bible to teach, convict, correct, or instruct your children—time that you would perhaps prefer to spend doing something else. And most of all, it takes time for children to grow up.

There is no such thing as instant maturity. There is no pill you can give them, no school you can send them to, no wiffle dust that you can sprinkle over them that will quickly transform their rebellious little hearts into obedient ones and bring them to maturity. Maturity takes time.

Progressive Sanctification

Another term for the process whereby Christians are transformed into the image of Christ is called progressive sanctification. It is called "progressive" because it occurs continuously throughout our lives rather than instantaneously (at one point in time). The Holy Spirit is the Principle Agent Who sanctifies, working in the hearts of all true believers to make them more like Christ. But He does so by *means* of the Word. A person simply cannot change in ways that are pleasing to God apart from the Word. The Holy Spirit must have His most effective weapon (the Sword of the Spirit) if He is to so change you and your children. Like regeneration,[1] sanctification is an act of God. But unlike regeneration, it is an act of God that requires your cooperation. The single most important way you can cooperate with Him is by getting the Bible into your heart. Then as a parent you must cooperate with His work in your child's life by getting the Bible into his heart.

I've met an astounding number of Christians who believe they can grow in grace apart from regular and continuous time in the Word (i.e., Bible reading, study, memorization, meditation, and active listening to Bible preaching and teaching). At the risk of overstating my argument,

---

[1] Regeneration is the instantaneous change in man's governing disposition (nature) that occurs as the Spirit of God gives new life to those who truly believe in Jesus Christ.

let me say it this way: It doesn't much matter how much time you spend in prayer or fasting, in fellowship with other Christians, in ministering or in witnessing to others; if you're not spending time in God's Word (or to be more accurate—if God's Word does not richly dwell in you), you are, for all intents and purposes, handcuffing the Holy Spirit. Oh, it's not that He is unable to work if you don't cooperate. It's that He has not promised to work apart from the Bible.

> That the Holy Spirit operates through the Bible is… confirmed in that what the Bible is said to do, the Spirit is likewise said to do. For example, each of the four functions of Scripture (listed below) is said to be performed also by the Holy Spirit (in the verses added):
>
> 1. "Teaching": compare I John 2:27 (the "anointing" represents the Holy Spirit).
> 2. "Conviction": compare John 16:7-11.
> 3. "Correction": compare Galatians 6:1; 5:22, 23.
> 4. "Disciplined training in righteousness": compare Galatians 5:16-18; Romans 6-8.
>
> In each case, the Spirit works by means of the Bible.[1]

A further indication of the Spirit's working by means of the Word can be seen by comparing the language of two parallel passages of Scripture. In Ephesians 5:18 we are commanded, "Do not get drunk with wine, for that is dissipation [that will lead to the disintegration of your life], but be filled with the Spirit." This verse is followed by a series of general instructions and directives addressed to specific individuals. These instructions and directives flow out of the initial command to be spirit-filled. These same directions can be found almost verbatim in the book of Colossians (3:16ff.) where they are not associated with the Spirit but with the Word. "Let the word of Christ richly dwell within you." (The chart on page 8 will help you do your own verse by verse analysis of these two passages.) In addition to demonstrating the close relationship between the Spirit and the Word, the

---

[1] Taken from *How to Help People Change* by Jay Adams, (Grand Rapids, MI: Zondervan Publishing House, 1986).

similarity between these two passages also provides insight into the means whereby He fills us. To the degree that a person allows the Word of God to fill his heart, the Spirit fills his life.

So if your want your children to be saved, sanctified and Spirit-filled, you must invest the time (up front) to train them with the Scriptures. Remember, the Spirit's fruit does not grow overnight but rather develops gradually as it is nourished with the Word of God. As we shall see in the pages that follow, according to the Bible it's your job to impress deeply upon the hearts of your children the Holy Scriptures which are able to make them wise about salvation through Jesus Christ.

Ephesians	Colossians
5:18 "Be filled with the Spirit."	**3:16** "Let the word of Christ richly dwell within you."
5:19, 20 "…be speaking to one another in psalms and hymns and spiritual songs, singing and making melody with your heart to the Lord; always giving thanks for all things in the name of our Lord Jesus Christ to God, even the Father;"	**3:16, 17** "…teaching and admonishing one another with psalms [and] hymns [and] spiritual songs, singing with thankfulness in your hearts to God. And whatever you do in word or deed, [do] all in the name of the Lord Jesus, giving thanks through Him to God the Father."
5:22 "Wives, [be subject] to your own husbands, as to the Lord."	**3:18** "Wives, be subject to your husbands, as is fitting in the Lord."
5:25 "Husbands, love your wives, just as Christ also loved the church and gave Himself up for her;"	**3:19** "Husbands, love your wives, and do not be embittered against them."
6:1 "Children, obey your parents in the Lord, for this is right."	**3:20** "Children, be obedient to your parents in all things, for this is well-pleasing to the Lord."

Ephesians	Colossians
6:4 "And, fathers, do not provoke your children to anger; but bring them up in the discipline and instruction of the Lord."	**3:21** "Fathers, do not exasperate your children, that they may not lose heart."
6:5-8 "Slaves, be obedient to those who are your masters according to the flesh, with fear and trembling, in the sincerity of your heart, as to Christ; not by way of eye service, as men-pleasers, but as slaves of Christ, doing the will of God from the heart. With good will render service, as to the Lord, and not to men, knowing that whatever good thing each one does, this he will receive back from the Lord, whether slave or free."	**3:22-24** "Slaves, in all things obey those who are your masters on earth, not with external service, as those who [merely] please men, but with sincerity of heart, fearing the Lord. Whatever you do, do your work heartily, as for the Lord rather than for men; knowing that from the Lord you will receive the reward of the inheritance. It is the Lord Christ whom you serve."
6:9 "And, masters, do the same things to them, and give up threatening, knowing that both their Master and yours is in heaven, and there is no partiality with Him."	**4:1** "Masters, grant to your slaves justice and fairness, knowing that you too have a Master in heaven."

Children should be taught early the important truths of God's Word. They should early be taught that there is a God; that He is a being of infinite power and wisdom, knowledge and goodness, justice, mercy, and truth, one God in three persons; that He is to be loved with all the heart, and obeyed in all things with the most dutiful respect; that His law is holy, just, and good; that all mankind are by nature sinners, and are exposed to everlasting destruction; that God has freely given His own Son to die for sinners, and to bring in everlasting righteousness for their justification; that everyone ought immediately to repent and embrace the Savior; that all the unconverted reject the mercy of God, and will continue to reject it to their eternal ruin; and that all who are thus renewed and made alive to God will be pardoned and sanctified, and finally received to honor, glory, and immortality.

These and other gospel truths connected with these should be taught to our children with diligence and faithfulness. They are truths which concern their eternal salvation. Nor are we to say that children cannot understand them; for it has been found by pleasing experience that, if proper means are used, children will very early get so much knowledge of divine truth as to be of the greatest benefit to them in all their future lives.

Samuel Worcester, D. D., October 1811[1]

---

[1] From his sermon "Parental Duties Illustrated," as reprinted in *The Godly Family: Essays on the Duties of Parents and Children* (Soli Deo Gloria Publications, 1993), pp. 81-82.

chapter two
Teaching the Scriptures

My goal in this chapter is to unpack a single portion of Scripture that you might see the profound implications it has on your life. In fact, if you're looking for something to powerfully motivate you to be a better parent, may I recommend that you commit this passage to memory. When properly understood there is probably no other portion of God's Word that consistently inspires parents to use the Scriptures in child training more than this:

> And these words, which I am commanding you today, shall be on your heart; and you shall teach them diligently to your sons and shall talk of them when you sit in your house and when you walk by the way and when you lie down and when you rise up. And you shall bind them as a sign on your hand and they shall be as frontals on your forehead. And you shall write them on the doorposts of your house and on your gates.　　(Deut. 6:6-9)

If you have been a Christian for any length of time, you're probably already familiar with the preamble to these three verses—you may have even committed them to memory already: "Hear, O Israel! The Lord is our God, the Lord is one! And you shall love the Lord your God with all your heart and with all your soul and with all your might" (Deut. 6:4, 5). "This," according to Jesus, "is the great and foremost commandment" (Matt. 22:37, 38). But what follows is perhaps the greatest and foremost commandment for biblical parenting. And that commandment has to do with teaching Scripture to your children.

The very first thing you are told to do as an expression of (if not a means to) your love for God is to internalize His Word yourself. Loving God and knowing His Word are inseparable—they are woven together as threads of the same fabric. "If you love Me," Jesus says, "you will keep My commandments." To the degree that you love and delight in God's Word (Ps. 119:24, 47, 48, 113, 127, 143, 159, 165 &

11

167), you will love and delight in Him. As we've already seen, to the extent that the Word of Christ dwells in you, you will be filled with the Spirit. To the measure you know the Scriptures, you will become wise unto salvation.

Have you ever heard this riddle? *Question:* What is the first rule for teaching a parakeet how to talk? *Answer:* You must have a larger vocabulary than the parakeet!

The same principle is true of parenting. If you (like Timothy's mother and grandmother) are going to teach your children God's Word, you must know the Scriptures yourself. There is no escaping it. There is no effective shortcut to studying the Bible yourself. Of course, you can read them stories from the Bible, anecdotes from a daily devotional quarterly, and catechize them from a catechism manual.[1] But as good as these methods are, they are not as effective as communicating biblical truth from your heart directly to theirs with personal insight and application. For you to rely solely on someone else's preparation of God's Word for your children is to neglect the first part of the passage before us (Deut. 6:6). Someone has said that a message prepared in a mind reaches a mind, but a message prepared in a life reaches a life. In other words, the more of God's Word you have internalized for yourself (v. 6) the more effectively you will be able to properly indoctrinate your children in the Scriptures (vv. 7-9). Your goal should be to increasingly become like one of the scribes Jesus speaks of in Matthew 13:52, who knows the Scriptures so well that he "brings forth out of his treasure things new and old,"—that is, things he has learned from others and things he has figured out for himself.

The phrase "shall be on your heart" is translated from two Hebrew words that mean "upon the inner man." Five chapters later God expands upon this internalization concept by adding a couple of inten-

---

[1] Catechizing children, when done in conjunction with the Scriptures, helps parents to fulfill Deuteronomy 6:6-9 in at least two ways. It is a means of impressing the Scriptures on the heart of your child, and (as your children learn the answers to the catechism questions they will generate other questions for you to answer biblically) it sets the stage for you to "*talk about them* when you sit at home and when you walk along the road, when you lie down and when you get up" (NIV).

sifiers. "You shall therefore *impress* these words of mine on your heart *and on your soul*" (Deut. 11:18). The word impress means "to put or place something somewhere." The something is Scripture, the someplace is your heart and your soul. God wants you to place his Word in your heart and in your soul.

What then are the means whereby you may impress these Scriptures on your heart? They are regular Bible reading and Bible study, biblical discourse (letting the word of Christ richly dwell within you involves "teaching and admonishing one another with psalms [and] hymns [and] spiritual songs," etc.), especially with your children ("and you shall…talk of them when you sit in your house and when you walk by the way and when you lie down and when you rise up"), listening to the teaching and preaching of the Word, and, perhaps most importantly, daily meditation on the Scriptures (which we shall study later). Yet beyond all of this, having God's Word on your heart means that the Scriptures are governing all areas of your life. When God's Word is on your heart, it affects your entire life.

Repeatedly, in the Bible, the heart (who a person is on the inside) is set over against the body and its members (what he does on the outside). The parallelism between the outward man and the inner man is hard to miss. The heart is connected to and contrasted with the flesh (Psalm 73:26), the hands (Ecc. 7:26), the feet (Prov. 6:18), the mouth (Psalm 19:14), the lips (Prov. 12:2), the tongue (Prov. 10:20), the eyes (Prov. 21:4), the face (Prov. 15:13), and even the neck (2 Chr. 36:13). This, in part, is why King Solomon said, "Watch over your heart with all diligence, For from it [flow] the springs of life" (Prov. 4:23). So when God says that His Word is to be "on your heart," He means that your whole life (inner and outer) is to be controlled by the Word.

Teaching the Bible is an Imperative

In the final analysis, it is not the responsibility of the pastor, youth leader, or Sunday school teacher to indoctrinate your children in the Bible. That's your job! Church leaders cannot always be with your children during those times when the Scriptures are to be taught ("when you sit in your house and when you walk by the way and when you lie down and when you rise up"). Even when they do augment your children's Bible education, they do so largely as your agent. "Now I say, as long as the heir is a child, he does not differ at all from a slave although he is owner of everything, but he is under guardians and managers until the date set by the father" (Gal. 4:1-2).

Teaching the Bible to your children is non-optional. You have been given the responsibility to indoctrinate your children with Scripture. The question is not whether or not you are going to teach God's Word to them, but whether or not you are going to obey God's Word yourself. No matter what you believe your parental job description entails, nothing else you do to, for, or with them is more important than this.

Teaching the Bible is an Explicit Imperative

Teaching the Bible to children is an explicit imperative for Christian parents. "You shall teach them diligently to [impress them deeply upon] your sons and shall talk of them when you sit in your house and when you walk by the way and when you lie down and when you rise up" (Deut 6:7).

In his book, *Back to the Blackboard*, Jay Adams unpacks the meaning of the most significant verb in this verse.[1]

> The word translated "impress deeply" in the Berkley version is a single Hebrew verb that means to "say something twice" (it is related to the number two). Then, it comes to mean "say it again" or "repeat." It is used of sharpening a sword because in the whetting process the blade is *repeatedly* struck or rubbed against the honing stone.... The second factor in the word moves away from the idea of repetition as merely rote learning, to the idea of applying truth to situation after situation to which it corresponds. Surely, one must learn the truth, but repeatedly he must show its application to everyday, real life circumstances. Truth must be integrated with life.

---

[1] Jay E. Adams, *Back to the Blackboard* (Woodruff, SC: TIMELESS TEXTS, 1982).

Children must be taught how the Scriptures relate to every area of life. The goal is not simply to teach the story of David and Goliath but also to explain how the narrative relates to the child's relationship with God, his parents, siblings, and schoolmates. You must teach not only the interpretation of each passage but also teach its application. Each passage of Scripture has only one interpretation which was intended by the Holy Spirit when He produced it through human authors (2 Pet. 1:20-21). But as the psalmist infers when he says, "To all perfection I see a limit; but Your commands are boundless" (Ps. 119:96, NIV), there are virtually no limits[1] to the application of Scripture to life.

Let's take, for example, the biblical command to "Do everything without complaining or arguing" (Phil. 2:14, NIV). Your task is to teach your child not only the meaning of the words *arguing* and *complaining*, but also how to apply it to a variety of situations that might occur in his everyday life.

- "You may not argue or complain when you don't like your breakfast."
- "You may not argue or complain when you have to stop playing."
- "You may not argue or complain when you are told to go to bed."
- "You may not argue or complain when you are told to do your homework."
- "You may not argue or complain when your will conflicts with the Lord's."

Teaching in the Milieu

Now, what exactly does it mean to teach and apply the Scriptures to your children "when you sit in your house and when you walk by the way and when you lie down and when you rise up?" Does God

---

[1] The application of properly interpreted Scripture passages is limited by other passages which may set the boundaries for certain applications. Scripture cannot be made to contradict Scripture. Hence, the Proverb, "It is better to live in a corner of the roof than in a house shared with a contentious woman" (25:24), is largely limited to "premarital" applications and cannot rightly be applied to a man who wants to divorce his wife on the grounds of her being a "contentious" woman since it would then contradict Matthew 19:2-6.

want you to schedule four daily catechism appointments with them? Not exactly. When you sit in your house and when you walk by the way and when you lie down and when you rise up means *everywhere!* Not only must you *teach* the Scriptures diligently to your children, you must also *talk of (or about) them* continuously. God wants you to teach and apply the Scriptures to your children in all kinds of places and in all types of circumstances, whenever and wherever life takes you. You are to teach in the *milieu* of life, addressing from the Scriptures the actual situations your children are facing morning, noon, and night. In other words, you are to discuss with your children the relevancy of Scripture not only *to* all of life's situations, but while you and they are actually *in* the midst of those situations. *Milieu* (Lit. *middle*) is a French word that means *environment* or *setting* or *surroundings.* While they are in the middle of life's circumstances, or when they are sur-rounded by them, is the best time to teach and apply the Scriptures to your kids.

Now, what exactly does it mean to "bind them as a sign on your hand, have them be as frontals on your forehead" and to "write them on the doorposts of your house and on your gates?"

Although some have tried to apply these verses literally, it is more likely they were intended to be taken metaphorically. We should teach our children that the Scriptures are to govern *all* of our behavior. To "bind them as [note the metaphor] a sign on your hand" speaks to the Scriptures governing our actions. "They shall be as [same metaphor] frontals on your forehead" implies that the Scriptures should govern our thoughts. Once again the message is clear: we should teach our children that the Scriptures are to govern *all* of life.

To "write them on the doorposts of your house" means that you are to use the Scriptures (cf. 2 Tim. 3:16) *"at home or in the city."* Whether you are going out the door to, or coming home from your daily activities, God's word has relevance to what you do. The command to "[write them] on your gates"[1] most likely makes reference to the necessity of applying the Scriptures not only when you are around

---

[1] Since it was at the gates that so many important decisions and business transactions were made, this might also have reference to the use of the Scriptures in social matters and business decisions.

your family and friends, but also when you are out of town. *Every-where* and in *all circumstances* the Scriptures are to be applied to life!

What are the Benefits of Teaching in the Milieu?[1]

We all learn better, faster, and more eagerly when we can see the value of what we are learning to our life (when we are personally motivated to apply the truth to our own life). It has always amazed me how my desire to learn some new truth is intensified when I realize how much I need it. What Solomon said of our physical appetite is also true of our spiritual appetite. "He who is full loathes honey, but to the hungry even what is bitter tastes sweet" (Prov. 27:7, NIV). God's Word never seems as relevant as when we are spiritually hungry—that is, when we recognize how much we need to be fed. Of course, we should read and study God's Word whether or not we're hungry, just as you should instruct your children in the Scriptures whether or not they seem interested. But when they are applied in the midst of life's providences, they are usually attended to and grasped more readily.

I never developed an interest in history when I was a child because I never understood how past history related to my present life. It wasn't until Bible college that I began to see the relevance of learning from the mistakes of others (i.e., that God could be glorified, and I could personally benefit from the study of heretofore boring facts about lots of dead people). As I began to relate those mistakes to specific violations of God's Word, history started to come alive for me. Of course, the same milieu principle holds to the biblically-based decisions that God's people made throughout history, which motivates me to follow their faith.

A few months ago I was driving my older daughter (then seven years old) to school. On the way she asked me a question: "Daddy, why don't we have cable television any more?" Our family had recently moved into a new house and after consulting with my wife, I had decided not to opt for the 40+ station cable television package that we had in our previous home. This, of course, had profound implica-

---

[1] Adapted from *How to Help People Change* by Jay E. Adams (Grand Rapids: Zondervan Publishing House), pp. 84-86

tions for Sophia, who really enjoyed some of the programming on several of those stations. Now, I could have given her a quick answer such as, "Mommy and I think it will help us make better use of our time if we aren't tempted to watch so much television." Except for the fact that it was really more of a temptation for "Daddy" than it ever was for "Mommy," that would have been a very truthful answer.

Instead of the short answer, I decided to give her a three minute Bible lesson on Christ's doctrine of radical amputation that went something like this:

"Sweetheart, Jesus said something pretty radical in His Sermon on the Mount. He said, 'If your right eye makes you stumble, tear it out, and throw it from you; for it is better for you that one of the parts of your body perish, than for your whole body to be thrown into hell. And if your right hand makes you stumble, cut it off, and throw it from you; for it is better for you that one of the parts of your body perish, than for your whole body to go into hell.' Do you know what that means?"

"Not really."

"Do you think Jesus wants us to literally cut off our hands and poke out our eyes?"

"Um…No?"

"Exactly. He really doesn't mean that we should intentionally harm our bodies."

"What does He mean then?"

"He means that we are to cut out of our lives anything that tempts us to sin against God. Daddy decided to not subscribe to cable television for a while until he can learn how to not waste so much of God's time. Maybe when I can learn how to be more self-disciplined with my time, we'll be able to have cable again."

By teaching her Matthew 5:29-30 in the context of her question about life and my own struggle with time management, she was more eager and interested in the Bible than she probably would have been if I had tried to teach her this truth during family time.

Family Time

"What," you might be asking yourself, "is family time?" In our household, we have instituted a tradition of family worship and Bible study which we call family time. This (almost) daily and somewhat casual activity takes place after the evening meal. Sometimes it takes place at the kitchen table, sometimes in the family room. It is a time when I teach the Scriptures to our daughters in a more formal way.

As with personal Bible study time, I believe "variety is the spice of life" when it comes to family Bible study. Consequently, we use a variety of Bible study methods during family time. Regardless of the methods, however, I endeavor to always teach in the milieu. Sometimes our Bible study is built around correcting behavioral issues in Sophia's life (and occasionally in my own life as well). I may, for example, be aware of a struggle she is having with a sinful attitude, action, or form of communication. Sometimes I ask Kim, "Is there anything in Sophia's life that we need to address tonight." Sometimes I ask Sophia if she's having any conflicts or problems in school with which she needs help. In all of these questions, the milieu is apparent and the appropriate Scriptures are applied immediately to her little life. (We've even sent her back to school with a Scripture verse printed on a piece of paper for her to minister to one of her little friends.) She knows that the Bible applies to all of life.

At other times, our family Bible study is more structured and therefore less naturally disposed to the milieu of her life. In such cases, I try to create the milieu for her. That is, after explaining and interpreting the passage in a book of the Bible or a topical study that we are learning, I try to help her see the different opportunities in her life that she may have to use it. I may, for example set up a potential scenario she might face at school: "How would this verse apply if you're taking a test at school and you notice that someone is trying to look at your answers for a little help?" Or perhaps I say, "Sweetheart, can you think of the last time someone embarrassed you by what he said to you in front of someone else? According to this verse what should you do?" I might ask, "What went through your mind when that happened? According to this verse, what could you have told yourself instead?"

Whether it is teaching the Scriptures to my wife and daughters, to a counselee, to my students, or to the congregation of our church, I endeavor to help my audience apply the Scriptures to life. I work hard at being creative. I take pains to insure that the Scriptures are understood in and applied to the context of everyday life. I do this by placing the Scriptures in the milieu of my disciples' lives.

To illustrate the impact of milieu teaching, I sometimes liken the heart of a child to a smooth non-porous surface such as a table top. My goal as a teacher is to have the child absorb as much of what I'm teaching as possible. If I were to pour the water of the Word onto that smooth surface, most of it would run off. But if I drilled hundreds of tiny holes in that surface (so that by the time I finished drilling it would be as porous as a sponge), then the water would be thoroughly absorbed into the table. Teaching in the milieu (showing how the Scriptures relate to the issues of actual life circumstances) is tantamount to drilling those tiny holes—it makes it easier for your child to absorb God's Word. It also leaves a more lasting impression. As sanding a piece of furniture before applying the stain prepares the wood to absorb more of the color, so preparing the child to receive the Word by showing him its relevance prepares him to absorb more of the truth.

Teaching to Observe

This leads us to the *second* benefit of teaching in the milieu. Not only do we learn better, faster, and more eagerly when we can see the value of what we are learning to our life, but we also are able to put what we are learning into practice immediately because we are learning for the purpose of doing.

The pluralistic society in which we live holds to a view of learning that is quite different from that of the Bible. Our secular society has adopted a *Greek* view of learning which believes knowledge should be sought for knowledge's sake. Knowledge to the average American is facts to be learned. Indeed, the humanist believes education itself to be the savior of mankind.[1] The idea seems to be amassing as much knowledge as one can in order to know more than the next person. Learning, in other words, for the average American is self-serving. The goal is to get as many letters after your name as possible so that

---

[1] See Appendix D: "The Fallacy of Humanism" (p. 149, noting especially #11).

you can get a good paying job so that you can find real satisfaction[1] in doing whatever you enjoy.

This self-oriented view of learning is antithetical to the biblical view. For the Christian, learning is not facts to be learned, but rather truth to be lived. It's not knowledge for the sake of knowledge, but rather knowledge for the sake of implementation. Jesus didn't say to the disciples when He gave the Great Commission, "teaching them *to know* all that I commanded," but rather, "teaching them *to observe* all that I commanded." He didn't say in Luke 11:28, "blessed are those who *know* the word of God," but rather, "blessed are those who *hear* the word of God, *and observe it*." Paul didn't say to Timothy, "the things which you have heard from me in the presence of many witnesses, keep to yourself and do not disclose to anyone unless you can use them to brag how much knowledge you have acquired." The things he taught him he was to entrust to faithful men, who were able to *teach others also* (2 Tim. 2:2). Christians are not to use what they learn for their own glory and personal benefit, but rather for God's glory and the benefit of others.

Doctrine (for which all Scripture is useful) is to be turned into living. It is to be translated by the Christian in cooperation with the Spirit's leading (cf. Rom. 8:14), into a change of life. Look at how Paul prayed for the Colossians (1:9-10):

> For this reason also, since the day we heard [of it], we have not ceased to pray for you and to ask that you may be *filled with* the *knowledge* of His will in all *spiritual wisdom* and *understanding*...

Why did he pray such a prayer? Was it so they might become puffed up with such knowledge? Certainly not! Paul wanted all of his disciples to know the Scriptures so well that their hearts would be a repository bursting (filled) with biblical data necessary to determine God's will for their lives. But it didn't end there. The ultimate purpose

---

[1] "Satisfaction in life" is another popular theme promoted by secular humanists. See Appendix D: "The Fallacy of Humanism" (p. 149, noting especially #s 4, 7, 12, and 15).

for this knowledge was to *live* (walk) in such a way (producing fruit) that would please and glorify God.

> …so that you may *walk* in a manner worthy of the Lord, to please [Him] in all respects, bearing fruit in every good work and increasing in the knowledge of God.

Teaching in the milieu gives you the opportunity to help your child translate the facts you are giving him from his mind to his mouth and to his lips and to his hands. It helps him become a *"doer* of the Word rather than a *hearer* only."* It is your job to make clear how the truth you are teaching is to be practiced experientially. Your child must be shown how to apply the Scriptures you are teaching to the various situations and circumstances in life.

Teaching in the milieu provides the conduit between the Scriptures he is learning and the life he is living. Do you remember the story of Helen Keller? As a child, she had the most difficult time learning much of anything. It wasn't until Annie Sullivan employed a milieu teaching device that her whole attitude and desire for learning radically changed.

One day, after Helen threw a tantrum over her inability to understand a lesson, she and Anne were walking in the country and came upon a well-house. In her autobiography, Helen recorded what happened next on this most momentous day of her life.[1]

> We walked down the path to the well-house, attracted by the fragrance of the honeysuckle with which it was covered. Someone was drawing water and my teacher placed my hand under the spout. As the cool stream gushed over one hand she spelled into the other the word *water*, first slowly, then rapidly. I stood still, my whole attention fixed upon the motions of her fingers. Suddenly I felt a misty consciousness as of something forgotten—a thrill of returning thought; and somehow the mystery of language was revealed to me. I knew then that "w-a-t-e-r" meant the wonderful cool something that was flowing

---

[1] Helen Keller, *The Story of My Life*, (New York: Lancer Books, Inc., 1968), pp. 36, 37.

over my hand. That living word awakened my soul, gave it light, hope, joy, set it free! . . . I left the well-house eager to learn.

Why did Helen leave that flower-covered well-house with a whole new attitude about life in general and learning in particular? It was because she understood for the first time that what her mentor was trying to teach her had to do with *life*. When she realized that the truth she was learning on one hand had to do with the things she was experiencing on the other hand, she became excited. Young Helen Keller's life was changed because she saw the relevancy of what she was learning to what she was experiencing.

If one little moment in Helen Keller's life could have such a profound impact, can you imagine the impact that habitual teaching in the milieu can have on your children when it is done in the power of the Holy Spirit?

Practical Considerations
for Teaching the Bible to Children

1. Milieu teaching opportunities may be extended beyond the moment of incidence. If your child asks you a question, or has an experience which you are not immediately able to relate to Scripture, do a little research and teach the passage retroactively later that day or perhaps the next. Depending on the age of your child, the milieu moment usually does not grow stale for a few days. Of course, the closer to the event you bring in the Scripture, the more lasting impression your teaching will likely make on your child's heart.

2. Be sure to use vocabulary commensurate with your child's ability to understand. (Eschew obfuscation.) Break down complex and abstract theological terminology into more age appropriate, easily understood, and concrete concepts. (i.e., Justification means when God looks at a Christian, He sees him just as if he has never sinned; Sanctification means becoming more like Jesus every day.)

3. Keep teaching sessions relatively short depending on your child's attention span. If more time is needed, schedule additional lessons later that day or the next.

4. Consider using role-play to apply the passage you're teaching. Have your child play the part of his friend (or teacher or sibling) and you play the part of your child. Encourage him to play the devil's advocate as you respond to his remarks so as to apply the passage you're teaching him.

5. Encourage him to ask questions about the passage. If you can't answer them, tell him that you'll have to do a little research and will get back to him with the answer shortly. (Then do your homework and keep your promise!)

6. Ask him to create (imagine) his own milieu in which he might have to apply the passage.

7. Teach in the context of a loving relationship with your child. One of the most important elements of parenting is having the right kind of relationship with your child. A good teacher will become personally involved with his disciple. A good parent will have a loving relationship with his child that includes plenty of one-on-one communication time. Of course, both parents should be personally involved with the child and work hard at cultivating such a warm relationship. Being aware however, that this is not always the case, and because women typically have more time with their children than do men, I've included Appendix E: "A Word to Wives" (p. 154), which I trust will provide some additional help and hope for you ladies.

8. Teach young children who are unable to read how to memorize Bible passages. Before bedtime, try reading (or quoting) a passage of Scripture to them repeatedly for several (7-12) nights. "The Lord is my Shepherd, I shall not want." Then begin leaving out a few words asking the child to fill in the word(s) you have omitted. "The Lord is my _____, I shall not want _____." Continue this exercise for several nights allowing the child to fill in more and more of the words. The Lord is ____ _____, I shall ____ _____." The Lord ____ ____ _____, I ____ ____ _____." Eventually, your child should be able to recite the entire phrase back to you without any coaxing on your part.

9. Consider using a variety of child-oriented videos, CDs and audio cassettes containing Scripture which has been set to music. These

resources can be quite effective in helping children internalize God's Word. They can also save you some time and make learning the Scriptures an enjoyable, almost effortless activity for your children.

You would count him unworthy the name of a friend who, knowing a thief or an incendiary to lurk in your family with a design to kill, or rob, or burn your house, would conceal it from you, and not acquaint you with it in his own accord. There is no such thief, murderer, incendiary, as sin. Silence or concealment in this case is treachery. He is the most faithful friend, and worthy of most esteem and affection, that deals most plainly with us in reference to the discovery of our sin. He that is reserved in this case is but a false friend, a mere pretender to love, whereas, indeed, he hates his brother in his heart.

David Clarkson

A foolish physician he is, and a most unfaithful friend, that will let a sick man die for fear of troubling him; and cruel wretches are we to our friends, that will rather suffer them to go quietly to hell, than we will anger them, or hazard our reputation with them.

Richard Baxter[1]

---

[1] Both citations taken from *The Golden Treasury of Puritan Quotations.*

chapter three
Convicting
With the Scriptures

The second step in the biblical procedure for using the Scriptures in child training (or for any other purpose) is *conviction*. Conviction flows out of teaching because teaching makes people aware of what God requires. Jay Adams comments on the relationship between teaching and conviction in *How to Help People Change*. For the purposes of our discussion, I have taken the liberty to replace the words "counselor" and "counselee" with "parent" and "child" respectively in this citation. (I highly recommend reading his entire volume, making similar replacements where appropriate, to supplement the contents of this book.)[1]

> There are times when conviction and teaching go hand in hand. So we must not think of them as mutually exclusive. In order to produce conviction, one may have to teach new material or reteach in new ways what the child has heard but has not yet converted from theory to practice. The parent may need to further clarify biblical truth and how it applies to the particulars of his child's situation. The Bible requires the parent to learn skills in order to bring about conviction.

Since your children were born sinners and their lack of conformity to and transgression of God's revealed will is endemic, effectively using the Scriptures to convict them of their sin is a necessary element of biblical parenting. In the final analysis, it is God's will (not yours) your children must obey. Ultimately, the Scriptures must be brought to

---

[1] *How to Help People Change* by Jay E. Adams, pp. 107-108. Adams' work is especially helpful in providing broader explanations of the theological presuppositions and exegesis on which this book is based.

27

bear on their consciences if they are going to be convicted of their sin against Him.

What is Conviction?[1]

Perhaps you're wondering why I've been using the word "conviction" throughout this book as an alternative to the word "reproof" (or *reproving*) which appears in the most popular English Bible translations of 2 Timothy 3:16. I've done so because it better describes the meaning of the original word.

What comes to mind when you hear the word *conviction*? There are three common ways in which this word is used in the English language.

1. A strong personal belief: "I have a conviction about bringing up my children in the discipline and instruction of the Lord."
2. Feelings of guilt about a sin of which one has not yet repented: "I'm under conviction for my addiction to nicotine."
3. The legal process of being found culpable for a crime: "The district attorney was delighted to get a conviction on three of the four indictments against the defendant."

How do you suppose the word conviction is used in 2 Timothy 3:16? (Or to put it another way, which of these three definitions for conviction would you say best describes the Greek word used by Paul in this passage?) The answer may surprise you. When I've asked this question in parenting classes, the majority of those who have the courage to answer get it wrong. You see, our feeling-oriented culture is so used to viewing guilt as a feeling rather than as culpability before a Holy God that most would choose definition number 2: the feelings of guilt associated with being found culpable. But, that is the wrong answer.

When addressing the Laodicean Church in Revelation 3, Jesus Christ said:

> I know your deeds, that you are neither cold nor hot; I would that you were cold or hot. So because you are

---

[1] *How to Help People Change*, pp. 111-118

lukewarm, and neither hot nor cold, I will spit you out of
My mouth. Because you say, "I am rich, and have
become wealthy, and have need of nothing," and you do
not know that you are wretched and miserable and poor
and blind and naked, I advise you to buy from Me gold
refined by fire, that you may become rich, and white gar-
ments, that you may clothe yourself, and [that] the shame
of your nakedness may not be revealed; and eye salve to
anoint your eyes, that you may see. Those whom I love
[or care for], I reprove [*convict*] and discipline; be zealous therefore, and repent.   (vv. 15-19)

To which kind (which definition) of conviction was Jesus referring
in verse 19? The conviction He was speaking of coincides with definition number 3: He was *prosecuting His case* against them. The lukewarm church had deceived themselves into believing that they were
rich when, in fact, they were poor. They had grown self-sufficient
("I. . . have need of nothing"). They needed to be convicted (convinced) of their sin because they did not know that they were
"wretched and miserable and poor and blind and naked." This is the
meaning of the word *convict* as it is used in 2 Timothy 3:16: to prose-
cute a case against another so that he is convicted for the crime which
he has committed. The Greek word *elegcho* carries with it the idea of
refuting an opponent to the point of *convincing* him (or if not him, then
at least others who hear the evidence) of his sin. It is substantiating and
proving that the charges made against the *lawbreaker* are true.

Everyone who practices sin also practices lawlessness;
and *sin* is *lawlessness*.   (1 John 3:4)

The Laodicean Church did not realize either the extent to which
they were sinning or the degree to which they needed to change. Your
children do not always realize the extent to which they are sinning.
Neither do they often realize the extent to which they must change.
You must help them comprehend these things and you must do so with
the Scriptures. You must learn how to use the Bible to convince your
little lawbreakers that they have broken God's law and that apart from
Christ they stand condemned.

"But aren't you trying to get me to do something that is God's responsibility? After all, isn't it the job of the Holy Spirit to convict people of sin?"

The Holy Spirit certainly does convict of sin (John 16:8), as do the Scriptures (2 Tim. 3:16). But God's ministers also are charged with the ministry of conviction. Paul commanded Timothy to "convict" those under his spiritual care with the Scriptures. "Preach the word; be ready in season [and] out of season; reprove [convict], rebuke, exhort, with great patience and instruction" (2 Tim. 4:2). He also told him to *convict* those church leaders "who continue in sin…in the presence of all, so that the rest also may be fearful [of sinning]" (1 Tim. 5:20). In fact, one of the qualifications for being ordained as a pastor in the first place is the ability to convict those who contradict sound doctrine (Titus 1:9). Moreover, in chapter 2 of his epistle (vv. 9-11), James used the law to *convict* his hearers of being lawbreakers. Bringing conviction, therefore, is a part of the responsibility of the ministry of the Word. Since, as we have seen, one of the most important tasks as parents is to minister the Word to your children, using the Scriptures to bring about conviction in their hearts is a part of your responsibility. You must learn how to effectively use the Word to appeal to the consciences of your little lawbreakers.

Of course, all three agents of conviction (the Spirit, the Word, and the minister of the Word) are sometimes necessary to bring about the desired result. But when ministering the Word, the human agent must do so under the power of the Holy Spirit for the desired conviction to be efficacious. God's Spirit may work in any way He chooses, but we ought to expect Him to work in accordance with the way He has said He would work in the Bible. For example, haphazardly dispensing Bible verses ripped out of context while in a state of sinful anger for the purpose of vindictively embarrassing your child, probably will provoke him to anger (Eph. 6:4) sooner than it will smite his conscience and bring him to repentance.

Why Is Conviction So Important?

To begin with, conviction is important because your child's relationship to God is dependent upon it. From the process of being drawn to Christ to the moment-by-moment fellowship your child will enjoy with Him, conviction of sin is going to be an essential part of his walk.[1] Indeed, "reproofs for discipline are the way of life" (Prov. 6:23).

Yet, in an attempt to help parents change their children's behavior, many Christian parenting books (videos, periodicals, broadcasts and seminars) neglect the most important reason for doing so: to please God. As much as you want your children to change for other "good" reasons—such as their long term health and happiness (or your short term health and happiness)—your supreme motive for raising your children according to the Bible is to be that they may please and glorify God. All other motives (and objectives) should be subordinate to this one. It's plain to see how, when such an important motive as God's glory is overlooked in a person's parenting philosophy, the use of conviction can easily be underutilized in (if not absent from) his parenting methodology. Allow me to amend Adams again:[2]

> No process of change [or philosophy of parenting] that ignores a child's relationship to God can succeed no matter what gimmicks are used to get what the child wants. When a parent attempts to change a child's behavior without first seeking change in his relationship with God, the result is merely outward, pharisaical behavior, just as displeasing to God as the original selfish behavior.

Conviction is important for another reason. It is a prerequisite to repentance and change. As I pointed out in the first paragraph of this book, your primary objective in parenting is to facilitate your child's conformity to the character of Christ. No child, born a sinner, can be changed into the likeness of Christ without first being convicted of his want of Christ-likeness. It's not that the transforming process is going to be completed before he leaves your home—indeed, it will not be totally completed until the Lord returns—but your job while he is still

---

[1] Ultimately, it is God (not man) who is sovereign over the conviction process. We are dependent upon God the Spirit to use the Word and any other means He chooses to convict us of anything.
[2] *How to Help People Change*, p. 10.

at home is to get him to the point that he understands how to continue the process once he leaves. To put it another way, your purpose as a parent is to train your child to leave home and *stand up* on his own. But though he leaves you and your spouse to become one flesh with his own, conviction will be his constant companion until the day he dies. And if he is to be truly Christ-like, he, himself will have to learn how to convict others.

As we've seen already, your child cannot repent (change his mind) without first being convicted of his sin. "Those whom I love, I reprove [convict] and discipline; be zealous therefore, and repent" (Rev. 3:19). As these words of our Lord suggest, conviction of sin is a prerequisite to repentance—it is part and parcel of the biblical disciplinary process. Of course, it is possible for someone to be convicted of his sin without following through to repentance. But it is not possible for a person to repent sincerely (from the heart) without first being convicted.

Sharpening Your Sword

There are two essential skills that must be cultivated to success-fully use the Scriptures to bring conviction to your child. The *first* skill has to do with your familiarity of the Bible. You must know which por-tions of Scripture may be used for each specific convicting purpose. You must know *what* the Bible says and *where* it says it. You must sharpen your spiritual sword by understanding what the Bible says about the sinfulness of the specific sins with which your child is strug-gling.

Have you ever heard this one? "Daddy (or Mommy), I can't eat my spinach (or beets, or turnips or whatever)!" What Scripture did you choose to use in this milieu? One that I have used not only with my older daughter but with countless "I can't" statements from my coun-selees is Philippians. 4:13, "I can do all things through Him who strengthens me."

"You can't say 'can't' as a Christian. If God says you must (obey your parents), you *can*. You can learn to do anything that He requires of you in the Bible."

"But Daddy, I don't *want* to eat my spinach."

"That's all right, honey. You don't have to *want* to eat it—you just have to eat it. God asks me to do lots of things that I don't want to do. The first thing I did this morning, I did against my feelings. I got out of bed and didn't really want to. The Bible says to those who have put their trust in Christ, '*it is now possible* to live the remainder of your time in the flesh *no longer following human desires*, but following the will of God' (1 Pet. 4:2, CCNT). As a Christian I don't have to follow my desires but can follow the Bible instead. And the neat thing is...*after* I do what the Bible says, I'm usually glad I did it and feel good about having done it—just like you probably will after you eat your spinach. When our will conflicts with God's will (when what we want to do is different from what God wants us to do), we should and can choose to do His will."

Have you ever caught your child in a lie?

"The reason I didn't tell you the truth, Dad, is because I thought I'd get into trouble."

"Son, when we are tempted to lie, it is almost always because we're afraid of the consequences of telling the truth. In this case, you were afraid you would be disciplined for your dishonesty. And that fear is certainly well-founded. You apparently feared the consequences of telling the truth more than the consequences of displeasing God, who says that 'lying lips are an abomination to' Him, 'but those who deal faithfully are His delight' (Prov. 12:22). The word 'faithful' in that passage may also be translated 'truthful.' Do you know what the connection is between being truthful and being faithful?"

"I don't think so."

"A person who is known for telling the truth is faithful. To be faithful is to be dependable, reliable and trustworthy. People tend to trust people who are truthful and tend to be suspicious and untrusting of people who are not truthful. The Bible says in the very same chapter (v. 19) 'truthful lips will be established forever, but a lying tongue is only for a moment.' You see, when you tell people the truth, it may hurt them momentarily. But, as much as it hurts when you tell the truth, it doesn't hurt nearly as much and for nearly as long as it does when you tell them a lie. Do you understand now why your lying is such a terrible thing from God's point of view? Do you understand the extent to which it affects your relationship to others? Do you see how, when you tell falsehoods, you fail to love God and fail to love your neighbor, thus breaking the two greatest commandments in the Bible?"

It may take some time to develop proficiency in knowing where to locate the appropriate passages, but in time it will be worth it. The process of doing the research will not only be personally beneficial to you in your own growth as a Christian, but it can also be quite an enjoyable activity. Let me encourage you by pointing out that since all children have their own unique but common patterns of sinning (cf. 1 Cor. 10:13), one passage of Scripture often "covers a multitude of sins." You can often get lots of mileage out of a handful of passages you have studied on a particular topic (i.e., selfishness, disobedience, disrespect, discontentment, etc.). Perhaps the best way to encourage you at this point is to tell you that I have included an appendix (p. 131) with over 50 common inappropriate attitudes and behaviors to get you started in your training. There is also a selective bibliography of other resources which will help you locate additional passages. But more about that later.

Dispensing the Word vs. Ministering the Word

The *second* skill you must develop to effectively convict your children of sin is the ability to thoroughly explain the Scripture portions you are using. Just because the Bible claims that God's Word will not return to Him empty but will succeed in accomplishing His purposes (Is. 55:11), you should not have a casual attitude about your responsibility to use the Scriptures to convict. You cannot be content merely to dispense Bible verses like a Pez® dispenser dispenses candy (as though Scripture is some sort of magic pill that comes without instructions on the bottle). Men (and women) of God do not only tell their hearers what the Bible says; they also tell them what it means, and they tell them how to apply it to their lives. Your job as a parent is not to dispense Scripture but to minister it to the hearts of your children in the power of the Holy Spirit.

"Son, please tell me why you are angry?"

"I'm upset because Mom wouldn't let my friends come over and play with me after school."

"What did you do when she denied your request?"

"I started arguing with her."

"And then what happened?"

"That's when I got mad and said all those ugly things she told you I said to her."

"Why do you think you got so angry?"

"I don't know."

"I think I do. There's a passage in the Bible that asks and answers the 'why did you get angry' question."

"There is?"

"Sure! God gave us the Bible to teach us how to live a life that's pleasing to Him and correct our sinful ways of thinking and acting which make us miserable."

"Where does it tell me why I got so angry at Mom?"

"It's in the fourth chapter of the book of James. The Christians to whom James was writing were having such severe conflicts with each other that he had to rebuke them. He began by asking them to figure out where their anger was coming from. In fact, he used the language of war to describe what they were doing to each other. The question he posed to them is, 'What causes fights and conflicts among you?' Then he answers his own question. 'Don't they come from your *desires* that wage war inside of you?' You see, son, when we want something (some desire) more than we should, we can become sinfully angry. And it can be a good desire that gets us into trouble. Sometimes I've gotten sinfully angry at you because you didn't obey me."

"But isn't that good anger? Isn't it OK to get angry when someone does something wrong?"

"That depends on whether or not we get angry because the person sinned against God. Sometimes we get *more* angry because the person sinned against us than we do because he sinned against God. When that happens, it's probably sinful anger more than it is righteous anger."

"You mean, we can have both kinds of anger in our hearts at the same time?"

"That's right. Why do you suppose I sometimes send you to your room before I discipline you?"

"Because you're trying to get the bad anger out of your heart first?"

"Exactly."

"You see, it's our desires that get us into trouble. When we want something so much that we're willing to sin in order to get it, or sin (by getting angry) because we can't get it, then what we want—even if it's a good thing (like wanting our children to obey us or wanting to play with our friends)—we want too much. It was their inordinate *desires* that caused those early Christians to whom James was writing to fight and quarrel with each other."

"What does inordinate mean?"

"It means 'too much.' The term in this passage 'to wage war' is another military term. We might say it's like a soldier who digs a trench in the ground and hides there to protect himself from the enemy. Sometimes our desires can get so 'dug in' to our hearts (or as James says, 'members') that they become like little idols we don't want to give up. So when someone tries to take them from us or keeps us from having them, we get sinfully angry."

"I guess I got angry at Mom because she kept me from playing with my friends."

"What would you call the specific desire that caused all this trouble?"

"I don't know that it has a name."

"I wouldn't be so sure."

"What do you mean?"

"Some time ago, I made a little list of the things in my life about which I became angry. When I finished my list, I noticed that there were two kinds of things (two categories) into which almost everything on my list fell. The first one was money. I would get angry whenever anyone would mess with my money. And then I realized that the Bible did have a name for my sinful desire."

"What does the Bible call it?"

"In 1 Timothy 6:10, the Bible calls it 'the love of money' which is 'a root of all sorts of evil.'"

"That's neat! Not that you were a 'lover of money,' but that the Bible nailed you that way! What is the name of the other wrong desire you told me about?"

"That one is even worse because I was starting to become like a kind of person the Bible speaks about who has a serious problem."

"What do you mean?"

"Well, when a person continually practices the same sin over and over again, that sin kind of ... well, overtakes him. It starts to control him little by little, until at some point, God actually refers to that person by the name of the sin that has overtaken him."

"I still don't understand ... exactly."

"What does God call an individual who lies all the time?"

"A liar."

"How about someone who makes lots of foolish decisions?"

"A fool. I get it now. So what was the sin that started to overtake you?"

"I used to get really angry when other people wasted my time— especially my spare time. You know ... the time I *wanted* to spend fishing and hunting and just relaxing with the family. I believe I was starting to become a 'lover of pleasure' to which both the Old and New Testaments make reference."

"That's really neat. The way you figured that out, I mean."

"Thanks, but I really can't take credit for figuring it out. God's Spirit used the Bible verses I had memorized to convict me of my selfishness, and He is giving me the grace to repent of these inordinate desires. Now, son, I'd like to ask you that question again."

"Which question."

"The one about the name of your sinful desire. Could it be, that the reason you got so angry at Mom is because you loved the *pleasure* of playing with your friends more than you loved (the pleasure of obeying) God? Could it be that you are starting to become what the Bible refers to as a *'lover of pleasure'*?"

With a little time, effort, and practice you can learn how (and develop the necessary skills) to find, explain, and apply the appropriate Scripture verses that God's Spirit can use to "convict" your children. They have need to be convicted not only of their sin but also of their need to trust Christ as Savior and Lord and to depend on the Holy Spirit for the grace necessary to live a life that is pleasing to the Father.

Additional Considerations About Conviction

Besides the two aforementioned skills, there are a few other practical factors to consider in using the Scriptures for conviction.

1. Examine your motives.

According to Galatians 6:1, the goal you're trying to accomplish when dealing with a brother who has been overtaken by a fault should be restoration. "Brethren, even if a man is caught in any trespass, you who are spiritual, restore such a one..." The word *restore* is a medical term used to describe the setting of a bone that has been broken. The idea is to make a person who has been overpowered by a sin useful again. We'll take a closer look at this word later, but for now suffice it to say that your motive should be to *restore* your child, not to expose him, make things easier for yourself, or extract personal vengeance on him by humiliating him. You may not use the parental authority God has given you for His glory and the benefit of your children for such selfish purposes as your own glory and personal benefit. As I alluded to earlier, don't try to convict your child of sin when you are more angry because he has sinned against you than you are because he sinned against God. This, in part, is what Paul meant when he added the words "looking to yourself, lest you too be tempted" to those he had charged with this restorative injunction. "Hypocrite," you'll remember, is the word the Lord Jesus uses to describe those who don't examine their own "log" before speaking to another about his "speck" (Matt. 7:3-5).

2. Use Biblical terminology when convicting children (or anyone else for that matter) of their sins.

When using the Scriptures to describe behavior, we ought to follow the example of Paul who spoke, "not in words taught us by human wisdom but in words taught by the Spirit, expressing spiritual truths in spiritual words" (NIV). To tell a child that he is too "shy" is not as likely to bring conviction as will showing him the relationship between his bashful behavior and the sin of *pride* and/or *rudeness* (to name just two). To refer to a son or daughter as "paranoid" does not smite his/her conscience as might biblical terms such as *fearful* or *suspicious*. Using the word "idiot" rather than "foolish" will more likely provoke him to anger than it will bring him to repentance. To say that "the evaluations you're making about yourself are not biblical (they're not true, honest, or right, etc.)" is much more theologically accurate (and hence convicting) than to say "you have a poor self-image." Of course, biblical terminology for irresponsible behavior smacks in the face of much of today's psychobabble which has reclassified what society used to call (and the Bible still calls) "sin" as "sickness." But biblical terminology is much more effective in helping children see their need to change. To help you in your quest to find the exact biblical terms you are looking for, Appendix A: "Scripture Texts for Child Training" (p. 131) has been included at the end of this book. Although far from exhaustive, it provides several Bible passages for over 50 common childhood behavioral problems and conditions.

3. **Argue your case so as to make it clear to the child that the indictment is for sins against God.**

Certainly, when a child sins against another individual he should be instructed to seek that person's forgiveness and, if necessary, make whatever further restitution is required biblically. But in the final analysis, sin is primarily against a thrice Holy God. After committing adultery with Bathsheba and murdering Uriah the Hittite, David said in Psalm 51:4, "Against Thee, Thee only, I have sinned, And done what is evil in Thy sight, So that Thou art justified when Thou dost speak, And blameless when Thou dost judge." The thrust of your arguments should not be, "Don't you realize how much you hurt me by what you did?" Your wording should rather focus on the severity of committing such a sin against God. "Do you know what God thinks about what you did? He tells us in the twelfth chapter of the book of Proverbs..." Now it is certainly not wrong to help children see exactly how their sin has affected others. Such appeals when rightly worded can be used by the Holy Spirit to bring conviction—as the one Nathan the Prophet used in his parable to David when he said in reference to Uriah:

> ...but the poor man had nothing except one little ewe
> lamb he had bought. He raised it, and it grew up with him
> and his children. It shared his food, drank from his cup

and even slept in his arms. It was like a daughter to him.
(2 Samuel 12:3, NIV)

Nathan effectively used King David's sense of justice and compassion to help him see how furious God was at his sin. Such appeals can be rightly used to bring conviction as long as they are ultimately aimed at showing the offender how he has sinned against God.

Children must understand not only that their sin is against God but that the standard of comparison is Jesus Christ as revealed in the Scriptures. Thus appeals to "behave like your brother" or "be respectful to your parents the way Sally is to hers" should be avoided unless they are being used to personify how the other person through his behavior is implementing a specific biblical principle or manifesting a particular Christ-like quality. The same principle holds true for all such "when I was your age" comparisons. As Paul told the Corinthians in reference to certain self-exalting false teachers, "when they measure themselves by themselves, and compare themselves with themselves, they are without understanding" (2 Cor. 10:12).

4. Choose the right time.

In the book of Ecclesiastes, King Solomon gives us two important insights which can be properly applied to the timing of conviction. First, in the seventh verse of chapter three he reminds us that "there is a time to keep silent and a time to speak." The best time to administer reproof is when you can secure the child's undivided attention. Sometimes my wife and I have handed our older daughter an abbreviated indictment to put an immediate end to wrong behavior only to come back later that evening when there was enough time to unpack all of the charges point by point in unabridged detail. As a rule, it is best to convict the child in private rather than in front of an audience. When a child sins in the presence of others, as Peter did in Galatians 2:14, a brief public rebuke may be beneficial—especially for those who have observed the sin.

The second applicable insight Solomon provides in reference to the timing of reproof is to not delay the process. "Because the sentence against an evil deed is not executed quickly, therefore the hearts of the sons of men among them are given fully to do evil" (Eccl. 8:11). This is especially important with younger children who may not be able to remember tomorrow what they did wrong today. Delay may give the impression that you believe the sin is not a very serious offense.

5. Choose the right words.

"The heart of the righteous ponders how to answer" (Prov. 15:28). It is often necessary to invest extra time, effort, and thought in selecting just the right words to express which biblical injunctions have been violated, which additional passages may be cited to support the indictment, the questions that will be asked of the child, and the manner in which the reproof will be administered (including such things as your spirit or attitude, the tone of your voice, and the way in which you may touch your child). Specific examples of the violation should be given—especially if a pattern of sin has developed.

6. Ask questions that appeal to your child's conscience.

The conscience is that organ of the soul which judges between right and wrong. It either accuses or excuses man's internal and external behavior to himself. Like an internal smoke detector, when functioning properly, it senses moral danger and sends out a discomforting signal to awaken us to our own culpability before God. The English word "conscience" and its Greek equivalent (*suneidêsis*) have the same basic etymological meaning: *with* (con/sun) *knowledge* (science/ eido). Thanks to the fall, your children came into the world with consciences that have been to some extent misprogrammed. Starting at infancy (2 Tim. 3:15), the process of reprogramming their consciences *with* the *knowledge* of Scripture must begin. This internal moral compass will need to be continually fine-tuned throughout your children's entire lives. Initially, you must provide the data which the Holy Spirit (the Master Programmer) can use to bring them to maturity. "But solid food is for the mature, who because of practice have their senses trained to discern good and evil" (Heb. 5:14).

When using the Scriptures for the purpose of conviction, you should take aim at the conscience of your child. You must try to disturb any complacency and indifference to sin and awaken him to the fact that he has done (or not done) something that is displeasing to God. You must provide him *with* the *knowledge* that he is once again in need of confessing and forsaking his sin and seeking God's forgiveness. This is what is I mean when I use the term "appeal to your child's conscience."

One of the functions of conscience is to make judgments about ourselves. You and I, if we're growing Christians, are continually in the process of judging or evaluating our behavior.[1] We ask ourselves questions like, "How am I doing in this area of my life?" "Am I pleasing God in that area?" "Am I succeeding over here?" "Where am I failing?" "What does the Lord want me to work on next?" When the answers to those questions confirm that we are conforming to God's revealed will for our lives, we have a good conscience and the peace that accompanies the knowledge that we are walking in obedience to Him. When the answers reveal that we are out of harmony with His will, our consciences smite us, producing conviction and the guilty feelings that accompany the knowledge of sin.

Because of the blinding effects of sin, our ability (and desire) to accurately judge ourselves has been weakened. Consequently, we sometimes need assistance with the evaluation process. We may need others to help us make the appropriate judgments about our behavior from time to time. That is where questioning comes into play. One of the most effective ways of awakening the conscience of others to their sin is by asking them questions. Certain types of questions put pressure on the conscience of those we convict by forcing them to examine themselves more closely than they might have done on their own.

The use of convicting questions can be seen throughout Scripture. They often begin with the word *why*. In Genesis 4:6 we read, "Then the Lord said to Cain, 'Why are you angry? And why has your countenance fallen?'" Pharaoh appealed to Abram's conscience in Genesis 12:18: "Then Pharaoh called Abram and said, 'What is this you have

---

[1] Unbelievers also evaluate themselves regularly. The problem is they do not do so exclusively according to Biblical standards. "For when Gentiles who do not have the Law do instinctively the things of the Law, these, not having the Law, are a law to themselves, in that they show the work of the Law written in their hearts, their conscience bearing witness, and their thoughts alternately accusing or else defending them" (Rom. 2:14, 15).

done to me? Why did you not tell me that she was your wife? Why did you say, 'She is my sister,' so that I took her for my wife?'"

After cutting off a piece of Saul's clothing, David secured a successful, albeit temporary, indictment against his King's conscience by posing a number of questions.

> And David said to Saul, "Why do you listen to the words of men, saying, 'Behold, David seeks to harm you'? Behold, this day your eyes have seen that the Lord had given you today into my hand in the cave, and some said to kill you, but [my eye] had pity on you; and I said, 'I will not stretch out my hand against my lord, for he is the Lord's anointed.' Now, my father, see! Indeed, see the edge of your robe in my hand! For in that I cut off the edge of your robe and did not kill you, know and perceive that there is no evil or rebellion in my hands, and I have not sinned against you, though you are lying in wait for my life to take it. May the Lord judge between you and me, and may the Lord avenge me on you; but my hand shall not be against you. As the proverb of the ancients says, 'Out of the wicked comes forth wickedness'; but my hand shall not be against you. After whom has the king of Israel come out? Whom are you pursuing? A dead dog, a single flea? The Lord therefore be judge and decide between you and me; and may He see and plead my cause, and deliver me from your hand." Now it came about when David had finished speaking these words to Saul, that Saul said, "Is this your voice, my son David?" Then Saul lifted up his voice and wept. (1 Sam. 24:9-16)

Jesus frequently used "why" type questions to convict his hearers.

"Why are you anxious about clothing?"   (Matt. 6:28)

"Why do you look at the speck that is in your brother's eye, but do not notice the log that is in your own eye?"
(Matt. 7:3)

"Why are you timid, you men of little faith?" (Matt.8:26)

"O you of little faith, why did you doubt?" (Matt. 14:31)

"Why do you yourselves transgress the commandment of God for the sake of your tradition?" (Matt. 15:3)

"Why are you testing Me, you hypocrites?" (Matt. 22:18)

"Why do you bother the woman? For she has done a good deed to Me." (Matt. 26:10)

"Why is it that you were looking for Me? Did you not know that I had to be in My Father's [house]?" (Luke 2:49)

"And why do you call Me, 'Lord, Lord,' and do not do what I say?" (Luke 6:46)

"You hypocrites! You know how to analyze the appearance of the earth and the sky, but why do you not analyze this present time? And why do you not even on your own initiative judge what is right?" (Luke 12:56, 57)

"Why are you sleeping? Rise and pray that you may not enter into temptation." (Luke 22:46)

"Why are you troubled, and why do doubts arise in your hearts?" (Luke 24:38)

"Did not Moses give you the Law, and [yet] none of you carries out the Law? Why do you seek to kill Me?" (John 7:19)

"Why do you not understand what I am saying? [It is] because you cannot hear My word." (John 8:43)

"If I speak truth, why do you not believe Me? He who is of God hears the words of God; for this reason you do not hear [them], because you are not of God." (John 8:46, 47)

As you can see by this modest sampling, the Bible provides you with plenty of insight on conviction through its many examples of conscience-pricking questions.

Now of course, "why" questions can be abused. They can be posed in sarcastic ways, asked punitively, or worded so as to elicit excuses, defensiveness, and justification rather than to bring conviction. For this reason, care must be taken and compassion demonstrated when using these type of questions. Keep in mind that Jesus avoided using "why" questions when He was seeking information, employing them almost exclusively to convict people of their sins. There are other interrogatives besides "why" that can be effectively used for conviction. I've included some examples of these in Appendix B: "Questions That Help Bring Conviction" (p. 144). I also strongly recommend that you do your own study of the various convicting questions found in the Bible to help strengthen your skills in this important area.

There are other ways in which you can appeal to your child's conscience besides asking questions. You can quote the appropriate biblical reference, read it to him or have him read it to you. You can construct a story or parable as Nathan did to David, and as Jesus occasionally did to His audiences. But whatever you do, remember to include the Scriptures, for they more than anything else are what the Spirit can use to awaken your child's heart to sin.

7. Comfort as you convict.

In six of the Revelation churches, our Lord began His message with praise and encouragement. Sincere praise and commendation serve to assure the child of your love for him. Since convicting little sinners of their sinfulness is a regular and continuous parental activity, the acclamation of your child's virtues should also be incessant. I recommend that parents keep their children bathed, as it were, in a solution of praise. My own personal goal, which I rarely achieve, is to commend my daughters (and wife) seven times for every reproof I administer. The key is not necessarily reducing the number of reproofs, but rather increasing the frequency and intensity of the approbations. When reproof is given to a child against this background, it helps ensure that he will develop a biblically accurate self-image (a balanced view of his strengths and weaknesses).

8. Give the reproof with a gentle spirit (Gal. 6:1).

Paul warns us to go "in the spirit of meekness." I've already explained the pitfalls of reproving your children when you are sinfully angry. Now I must warn you to exercise restraint when you are righteously angry. When our children sin against God, it may evoke in us righteous indignation. It is essential, however, that we do not express that holy passion in sinful communication forms. Of all the ways parents may misuse righteous anger, perhaps none is more common than scolding. In chapter two of my book *The Heart of Anger: Practical Help for the Prevention and Cure of Anger in Children* which identifies 25 specific ways parents typically provoke their children to anger, I've addressed this issue as follows:[1]

> And while He was in Bethany at the home of Simon the leper, and reclining [at the table], there came a woman with an alabaster vial of very costly perfume of pure nard; [and] she broke the vial and poured it over His head. But some were indignantly [remarking] to one another, "Why has this perfume been wasted? For this perfume might have been sold for over three hundred denarii, and [the money] given to the poor." And they were *scolding* her.   (Mark 14:3-5)
>
> One of the Greek words from which the term *scolding* (in the above text) was derived, means "to snort with anger." It was used to describe the snorting of horses. In his book *Hints on Child Training*, first published in 1891, H. Clay Trumbull, considered by many to be the founder of Sunday School, explains:
>
> "To 'scold' is to assail or revile with boisterous speech. The word itself seems to have a primary meaning akin to that of barking or howling.
>
> Scolding is always an expression of a bad spirit and of a loss of temper...the essence of the scolding is in the multiplication of hot words in expression of strong feel-

---

[1] *The Heart of Anger*, pp. 33, 34

ings that, while eminently natural, ought to be held in better control. It is scolding in the one case as in the other; and scolding is never in order.

If a child has done wrong, a child needs talking to; but no parent ought to talk to a child while that parent is unable to talk in a natural tone of voice, and with carefully measured words. If the parent is tempted to speak rapidly, or to multiply words without stopping to weigh them, or to show an excited state of feeling, the parent's first duty is to gain entire self-control. Until that control is secured, there is no use of the parent's trying to attempt any measure of child training. The loss of self-control is for the time being an utter loss of power for the control of others.

In giving commands or in giving censure to a child, the fewer and the more calmly spoken words the better. A child soon learns that scolding means less than quiet talking; and he even comes to find a certain satisfaction in waiting silently until the scolder has blown off the surplus feeling which vents itself in this way. There are times, indeed, when words may be multiplied to advantage in explaining to a child the nature and consequences of his offense, and the reasons why he should do differently in the future; but such words should always be spoken in gentleness, and in self-controlled earnestness. Scolding—rapidly spoken censure and protest, in the exhibit of strong feeling—is never in order as a means of training and directing a child."

Meekness (gentleness) is required when convicting others of their sin. When you are sinfully angry it is almost impossible to be gentle. Even when you are righteously angry, it is easy to be harsh. Prayerful pondering (cf. Prov. 15:28) is probably the best precaution you can take to insure your child will focus on the truth of your argument and not be distracted by your own struggle with anger.

There is one more component of meekness that I'd like to mention in reference to reproof. It has to do with humility. A truly meek person recognizes his own frailty and communicates that frailty in the process of reproving another. As I often tell my counselees, "I'm just one beggar telling another beggar where to find the bread. Next week you may be on this side of the desk reproving me and helping me with my struggles against sin." Or perhaps I say, "The things I'm telling you, I had to tell myself just last week." There is no tolerance for a "holier than thou" self-righteous attitude in the heart of a truly meek person.

Before concluding this chapter, I'd like to tell you about an imaginary plaque that hangs on the back wall of my office right between (and ten feet beyond) the two chairs in front of my desk. This make-believe work of art has embroidered upon it in big bold letters the words of Proverbs 28:23: "He who rebukes a man will afterward find [more] favor than he who flatters with the tongue." It's there to remind me that I must not get discouraged or distracted with the uncomfortable tension that often accompanies reproof—tension in my own heart and tension which I perceive in the voices and on the faces of those I reprove. It's there to give me hope that later on (if not at present), after the reproof has been given and the restoration has occurred, God will be most glorified,[1] and I will find favor in the eyes of my repentant counselee. Christian parent, don't let the attending discomfort associated with the ministry of conviction keep you from loving your child. Love him enough to give him what God says he needs—even if it's not what he wants!

---

[1] God will ultimately be glorified even if no repentance takes place when He executes judgment on the unrepentant.

Correct your son, and he will give you comfort; He will also delight your soul.

Proverbs 29:17

chapter four
Correcting
With the Scriptures

We come next to the third step in God's process of bringing about change in our children by means of His Word: correction. The Bible not only has power to convict, but it also has power to correct. It not only can diagnose spiritual disorders, but it can also remove malignancies and extricate the heart from entangling vestiges of corruption. The word correction (Gk: *epanorthoso*) means to stand something up or to make something stand again. We might say "to put back on one's feet." As a parent, you should know how to use the Scriptures not only to expose the sin in your children but also to put them back on their feet. With Bible in hand (or better still, on your heart), you must function not only in the capacity of prosecuting attorney but also as a skillful physician of the soul who is thoroughly equipped (2 Tim. 3:16) to treat spiritual maladies—even performing "corrective surgery" if necessary.

To correct something is to rectify it—to *make right* that which is or has gone wrong. Like the word admonish (Gk: *nouthesis*—the word from which the model of counseling I subscribe to is derived), correction presupposes the existence of some problem which needs to be straightened out. The Bible is useful for straightening out what is wrong in your child's life. Whether he started out on the wrong track (as every child does) or has been derailed and is unable to get to his destination, the Scriptures can pick him up and set him back on the right track. They provide you with all the necessary equipment to help correct any attitudes, actions, thoughts, and motives in your children that are not in accord with the character of Christ.

Looking closer into the concept of correction, we find there are several key components to this step that require some explanation. They are repentance, confession, forgiveness, forsaking sin, restitution, and restoration. (Keep in mind that although these elements are

51

distinct, they do overlap at some points. The walls between some of them do not extend all the way up to the ceiling.) The first term is repentance.

What is Repentance?

The problem with you and me is sin. The solution is Jesus Christ who came to do away with our sin. Legally, Christ did away with the eternal consequences of our sin by dying in our place on the cross. By so doing, He paid the price for the punishment of our sin, which satisfied God's wrath so that we could be justly forgiven. Practically, He does away with our sin by enabling us, through the Spirit, to become more like Himself. This process of sanctification involves change. And change is what repentance is all about.

The word repent literally means "to change one's mind." This is where correction begins. The initial result of having been convicted is a change of mind. Changing your mind is the first step toward changing your life. You realize that what you have been doing (or not doing) is wrong and must be stopped (or begun). As a result, you desire to change the direction of your life. You may or may not have strong feelings of remorse or sorrow,[1] but if you are repentant, you will at least regret the fact that you have sinned against God. But more importantly, if you are truly repentant you will start to see the fruit appropriate to repentance: a change that manifests itself in your lifestyle. Repentance, then, is changing your mind about your beliefs, attitudes, and behavior. It involves regret concerning your sin and produces a change in your lifestyle as outward evidence of your desire to be different.[2]

The Bible is a necessary part of this process because it provides specific information about the changes that must be made. It is the manual for enabling Christians to become more like their Lord. It is, therefore, the ultimate textbook on child training. But the Bible is more than that. It is an essential element of the parenting process. You

---

[1] The word for repentance is *metanoia*. It does not necessarily involve feelings of sorrow or remorse. The word for the feelings of sorrow over the consequences of one's actions (but not necessarily sins against God) is *metamelomai*. The two are often confused.

[2] *How to Help People Change*, p. 144.

cannot bring your children to genuine repentance without it. The Spirit applies the Word to the heart of your regenerate child[1] and produces fruit. This is why you must explain to your child the biblical basis for whatever is done in the process of correction. It is for this reason also that you must get your child into the Word; or better yet, get the Word into your child. Remember young Timothy! Keep in mind also that when you take your children through the various elements of correction, you are doing so, in part, with the hope of training them to learn how to someday do these things themselves (not at your behest and assistance, but totally at the leading of the Spirit). "For all who are being led by the Spirit of God, these are sons of God" (Rom. 8:14). Ideally, long before your child leaves home he will be more dependent on his Heavenly Father's leading (a term which, in context, speaks not of an internal *ad hoc* guidance counselor who gives direction for every circumstance in life but of God's supernatural empowerment in the progressive sanctification process), than he is on yours.

Fruit of repentance was the tangible evidence John the Baptist was looking for in the lives of those to whom he preached the baptism of repentance. After charging them to "bring forth fruits in keeping with repentance," he gave specific things to do to specific individuals who asked what they could do to demonstrate that they had, in fact, repented (Luke 3:8-14). To the man who had two tunics he said, "Share with him who has none." To the tax collectors he said, "Collect no more than what you have been ordered to." And to the soldiers he said, "Do not take money from anyone by force, or accuse [anyone] falsely, and be content with your wages."

In much the same way, you must explain to your child *from the Scriptures,* in specific concrete terms, what it is God requires of him if he is to repent of the sin for which you have convicted him. It is not enough to simply correct him by saying, "You've got to stop wasting so much time after school and work harder on your homework." You will have to do more than that to correct him biblically. You may find it necessary, for example, to show your child from the Bible the impor-

---

[1] If your child is not a Christian, you must, of course, use the Word to show him how a Christian changes. His failure to change becomes an opportunity to proclaim the gospel and show him his need for Christ.

tance of "redeeming the time," reminding him that if God, who is per-fect, runs His affairs according to a schedule, it would be unwise to believe that he can get by without one. You might require him to make a list of all his domestic and scholastic responsibilities in preparation for writing his own schedule. You can sit down and assist him with the schedule or perhaps let him assist you as you write the first draft. You may even ask him to interview his teachers for the purpose of ascer-taining how much time each recommends to be set aside on a weekly basis for homework and study. You may require him, at first, to let you hold him accountable on a daily or weekly basis for implementing the new schedule. And you should be prepared to explain the biblical directives and principles behind each of the corrective procedures you're giving him. This is the kind of specificity that biblical correc-tion involves. Correcting children in general terms does not often pro-duce the kind of fruit Christian parents long to see and, more importantly, the kind that is pleasing to God.

What About Confession?

The word confession in the New Testament (*homologeo*) literally means "to say the same thing." After your child has been successfully convicted of his crime, he will be in agreement with the case you've made against him. He will agree with the indictment and acknowledge (confess) in some way that he has truly sinned against God. He will say the same thing about his sin that you (and God) have been saying. And since the activity of confessing is made with the mouth (cf. Rom. 10:9, 10), he should confess his sin to *all* the appropriate parties—that is to God, to you, and to anyone else who might have been wronged by his transgression. The essence of confession, then, is a willingness to plead guilty before all the offended parties to the wrong for which one has been accused.[1]

---

[1] In the context of our discussion, the parent as the prosecuting attorney is accusing the child. When the Spirit convicts the child directly, the Scriptures themselves accuse him. So, even in self-imposed confessions, the sinner stands accused and must plead guilty as charged.

The purpose of confession is not primarily to relieve oneself of the feelings of guilt. It is, rather, to acknowledge one's culpability to those against whom he has sinned so that he might seek their forgiveness and be reconciled to them. As in conviction and repentance, specificity is essential. So also is the need to call sin by its right name. General confessions, such as "I know what I did wasn't right," don't make the grade. "While you were asleep, I stole six dollars and fifty cents from your purse," is a specific confession which contains the two essential ingredients. This brings us to the next component of correction: forgiveness.

What is Forgiveness?

Once the confession has been made, forgiveness must be sought by the child from all offended parties. Saying, "I'm sorry," is not enough. It doesn't tie up all the loose ends which must be mended to bring about reconciliation. In response to "I'm sorry for what I did," the offended party might say "I'm sorry you did it, too," or worse, "You are sorry—you're one of the sorriest people I know!" In either case, the matter remains open and reconciliation between the offender and the offended is not achieved. Apologizing (merely saying I'm sorry) does not secure the promise of forgiveness from the offended party. When God forgives us He promises to not remember our sins against us. "I will forgive their iniquity, and their sin I will remember no more" (Jer. 31:34). Jesus made it quite clear that it is a most serious transgression for a Christian to refuse to forgive someone who repents (Matt. 18:21ff.; Luke 17:3-10). Asking forgiveness forces the issue (are you going to do what the Bible says and forgive me or aren't you?). It puts pressure on the offended to be reconciled and closes the books on the whole matter. As confession is made to all offended parties, so forgiveness must be sought from all those who have been offended, beginning with God.

What about asking God's forgiveness? As Christians aren't we already forgiven? In providing them with a pattern for prayer, the Lord taught his disciples to pray, "forgive us our debts, as we also have forgiven our debtors" (Matt. 6:12). When we become Christians, God covers all our sins (past, present, and future) under the blood of Christ.

At that point, God's relationship with us changes so that He no longer relates to us primarily as a judge but rather as a loving Father. When we sin, we displease God and can no longer enjoy fellowship with Him until we deal with our sin. As the *Westminster Confession of Faith* so aptly puts it:

> God doth continue to forgive the sins of those that are justified; and, although they can never fall from the state of justification, yet they may, by their sins, fall under God's fatherly displeasure, and not have the light of His countenance restored unto them, until they humble themselves, confess their sins, beg pardon, and renew their faith and repentance.[1]

Confession and repentance go hand in hand. "If we confess our sins, He is faithful and righteous to forgive us our sins and to cleanse us from all unrighteousness" (1 John 1:9). There can be no forgiveness without confession, and there can be no enduring correction (or cleansing from unrighteousness) without first sweeping away the debris from past sin. To attempt to correct a child without repentance, confession, and forgiveness is as futile as trying to build a skyscraper on a foundation of sand. Perhaps the best way to begin teaching your children how to love God and how to love their neighbor is to teach them early about these first three important elements of correction.

Restitution: The Missing Ingredient

The biblical doctrine of restitution is rarely spoken of today. To some, it is little more than an Old Testament relic which, under grace, has been relegated to mothball status in today's New Testament grace-oriented Church. Nothing could be farther from the truth. While it is true that you and I could never repay the debt we owe to God for our sins, the requirement to pay back our debts to others *where possible* has not been rescinded. There are a significant number of Old and New Testament passages that deal very specifically with restitution (Ex.

---

[1] Morton H. Smith, *The Westminster Confession of Faith* (Simpsonville, SC: Christian Classics Foundation, 1997).

21:30-36; 22:1-4; Lev. 6:2-5; 24:18; Num. 5:7; 2 Sam. 12:6; Prov. 6:30, 31; Job 20:18; Ezek. 33:15; Luke 19:8; Philemon 10-20).

Commenting on section six of the *Westminster Confession of Faith*, A. A. Hodge explains:

> This section teaches...that when a Christian has personally injured a brother, or scandalized by his unchristian conduct the Church of Christ, he ought to be willing, by a public or a private confession, as the case may be, to declare his repentance to those that are offended, is also a dictate alike of natural reason and of Scripture. If we have done wrong, we stand in the position of one maintaining a wrong until, by an expressed repentance and, where possible, redress of the wrong, we place ourselves on the side of the right. The wrong-doer is plainly in debt to the man he has injured, to make every possible restitution to his feelings and interests; and the same principle holds true in relation to the general interests of the Christian community. The duty is expressly commanded in Scripture (Matt. 5:23, 24; Matt. 18:15-18; James 5:16).[1]

When children have stolen or destroyed property, injured the reputation of another, or committed any other sin in which those who were sinned against lost something, correction involves making restitution. Asking forgiveness in such cases is not enough. A willingness to do such things as pay for or replace broken toys, return to the owner that which was stolen, or make right a lie that was told, demonstrates genuine repentance. Of course, the appropriate passages of Scripture (or at least some reference or reminder that restitution is in accordance with God's will) should be cited or reviewed to underscore that what you are requiring of the child is no less than what God, Himself required.

---

[1] A. A. Hodge, *The Confession of Faith* (Simpsonville, SC: Christian Classics Foundation, 1997).

Forsaking (Putting Off) Sin

In Proverbs 28:13 we find another interesting word: "He who conceals his transgressions will not prosper, But he who confesses and *forsakes* [them] will find compassion." The Hebrew term (*azab*) is quite strong. It means to let go of, leave, forsake, or abandon. Sin must be let go of, left behind, abandoned and forsaken. Unwillingness to let go precludes God's blessing and short circuits the process of correction. It is naive to expect God to step aside and allow someone to prosper toward his goal until he lets go of the sin to which he is clinging.[1]

The concept of forsaking or letting go of sin corresponds to the New Testament idea of "putting off" sin. It is the first half of the two-fold change process essential for correction. (The second step closely approximates "disciplined training in righteousness" and will therefore be addressed in the next chapter.) I have previously outlined the put-off/put-on dynamic in my book *The Complete Husband*.[2]

Zap Theology: The kiss and make up with God syndrome

Have you ever struggled to overcome a bad habit in your life? Sure you have! We all have. Many Christians, however, when they "struggle" with sin don't really struggle at all. Rather, they simply confess their sin to God, pray that He will help them change, and promptly get off their knees expecting that God has somehow infused ("zapped") them with a special measure of grace which will enable them to never commit the same sin again, without any (or very little) further effort on their part. This is what is sometimes referred to as "the kiss and make up syndrome with God."[3]

Progressive sanctification is, of course, an act of God, but it is also a process which requires our cooperation. It is not enough merely to pray that God will change us. We must also *do* what the Bible says is

---

[1] *How to Help People Change*, p.154
[2] Lou Priolo, *The Complete Husband* (Amityville, New York: Calvary Press, 1999), pp.160-161.
[3] This term was used by Jay E. Adams in various lectures and personal conversations I've had the pleasure of having with him.

necessary to "put off" the sin and "put on" Christ. Change is a twofold process for the Christian. We actually put off our sin by putting on its biblical antithesis. To put it another way, Christians don't "break" habits—pagans do. Christians replace bad habits with good ones.

It is not enough for the Christian who habitually lies to simply stop lying. He must make it his goal to become truthful. "Therefore, laying aside falsehood, speak truth, each one [of you], with his neighbor, for we are members of one another" (Eph. 4:25). It is not enough for a thief to simply stop stealing. He must not only put off *stealing*, but he must also put on *diligence* and *generosity.* "Let him who steals steal no longer; but rather let him labor, performing with his own hands what is good, in order that he may have [something] to share with him who has need" (Eph. 4:28).

This put-off/put-on dynamic can happen only as the mind is renewed through the Scripture.

> That, in reference to your former manner of life, you lay aside the old self, which is being corrupted in accordance with the lusts of deceit, *and that you be renewed in the spirit of your mind,* and put on the new self, which in [the likeness of] God has been created in righteousness and holiness of the truth. (Eph. 4:22-24, emphasis added)

The Word of God is necessary to produce lasting change in your life. The Holy Spirit takes the Scriptures you have internalized (through Bible reading, study, memorization, meditation, etc.) and changes (transforms) you from the inside. "And do not be conformed to this world, but be transformed by the renewing of your mind, that you may prove what the will of God is, that which is good and acceptable and perfect" (Rom. 12:2). You cannot properly be sanctified apart from God's Word.

What is Involved in the Forsaking of Sin?

The first essential of forsaking, or putting off sin is self-denial. The child who is being corrected with the Scriptures must be confronted with the fact that his selfish desires (both those which are inherently sinful and those which are sinful, because they are inordinate) must be denied. He must be willing to say "no" to them. Getting children to practice self-denial is admittedly a challenge, to say the least. There are, however, some practical things you can do to help motivate them.

First, key concepts from Scripture passages can be explained to the child depending on his ability to comprehend them. Portions such as Galatians 5:16-24, "But I say, walk by the Spirit, and you will not carry out the desire of the flesh...those who belong to Christ Jesus have crucified the flesh with its passions and desires," and Romans 8:13, 14 "for if you are living according to the flesh, you must die; but if by the Spirit you are putting to death the deeds of the body, you will live," are especially helpful in demonstrating the need for Christians to depend upon the Holy Spirit's enabling power to forsake sin.

Secondly, teaching him to pray daily that the Lord will give him the wisdom to identify his sinful desires, and the grace to forsake them and replace them with alternative God-honoring desires, will help keep the issue of his own sinfulness before him, and hopefully the James 5:16 dynamic will prove effective ("the effective prayer of a righteous man can accomplish much").

Thirdly, talking to him regularly about the thoughts and motives behind his words and actions can be tremendously fruitful. I began doing this with my older daughter when she was two years old.

"Sophia, you seem to a have a pretty bad case of the 'wantas' today."

"Daddy, what do you mean?"

"You wanta do this and you wanta do that." Those wantas really get you into trouble."

"How?"

"Sometimes you want to do what *you* want to do more than you want to do what *God* wants you to do. That's not good!"

Questions like "What goes through your mind when you feel that way?" or "What is it you want or long for when you do that?" can uncover individual as well as patterns of sinful desires. Once those desires are exposed, biblical alternatives can be discussed ("What would have been a more God honoring thought/desire than the one you had?"). In *The Heart of Anger*, I've devoted two chapters to help parents do this very thing through the use of a biblically-based tool, which I refer to as a "Heart Journal."

Fourth, reminding him regularly that one of the reasons God allows Christians to go through trials is to reveal to them what kind of evil still exists in their hearts may help your child to look at self-denial in a new light. Or as my friend Sid Gallaway puts it, "God allows [trials so that their]...pressure against our flesh will squeeze our sinful hearts until the pus of selfishness comes to the surface and reveals how depraved we really are."

Fifth, training children at an early age to be obedience-oriented rather than feeling-oriented is one of the most effective practical recommendations I can make concerning self-denial. One evening during family time, we were talking about the necessity of choosing to obey God when our feelings tempt us to disobey. After I explained the difference between feeling-orientation and obedience-orientation, I asked Sophia (who was no more than five years old) to tell me what we should do when God asks us to do something we don't feel like doing. Her answer caused my wife and me to burst out in laughter. "I guess," she said, "we just have to hurt our feelings." For the moment, at least, she got the point.

The Doctrine of Radical Amputation

The next essential of forsaking or putting off sin has to do with removing from one's life anything (activities, situations, persons, etc.) that is a stumbling block. If a person is serious about breaking with sin, he will willingly remove those things that tempt him to continue in sin. This teaching is sometimes referred to as "the doctrine of radical amputation." You've already seen how, on at least one occasion, I taught this doctrine to my seven-year-old daughter. In His Sermon on the Mount (Matt. 5:29-30), after explaining to the disciples that lusting for a woman was, from God's point of view, adultery of the heart, Jesus said:

> If your right eye makes you stumble, tear it out, and throw it from you; for it is better for you that one of the parts of your body perish, than for your whole body to be thrown into hell. And if your right hand makes you stum-

ble, cut it off, and throw it from you; for it is better for you that one of the parts of your body perish, than for your whole body to go into hell.

He tells them that they must remove whatever makes them stumble into sin, even if it is something very important to them, like their right (best) eye or their right (best) hand. Sometimes things that are considered good or profitable (such as computers, school activities, or even certain types of food) may have to be eliminated (at least temporarily) until the child develops a greater degree of self-control. As a parent, you certainly have the authority to perform radical amputation on those things in your child's life that need to be removed. Indeed, for his own protection, you may in certain circumstances have a responsibility to do just that. But in my judgment, because our goal as parents is to teach our children how to apply the Bible to their own lives, it seems best to first give the child an opportunity to remove any provisions for defeat on his own. If you do find it necessary to impose the removal of certain stumbling blocks yourself, be certain to explain the biblical basis of doing so.

This brings us to the third essential of forsaking sin: putting a structure in place that will make it difficult to relapse into sin. Radical amputation not only eliminates opportunities to sin, it also unconsciously makes sinning much more difficult. Sinning after radical amputation requires a lot more deliberation and effort than it did before. The idea behind restructuring one's life is to put a person in a situation that would require him to go out of his way to sin.

Accountability

Accountability is yet another key to this element of forsaking sin. If your child is accountable only to himself, he may wrongly conclude that he has to answer only to himself. But if he is also accountable to you—especially for those sins he is needing to forsake, you can keep the importance of this matter before him. Additionally, the awareness that you could be asking him to give an account of his progress at any moment should be a strong deterrent to give in to temptation. There is much in the next chapter that could rightly be placed here. But such things must be set in a broader context. For the moment then, suffice it to say that, as a rule, the more difficult you make it for your child to fall back into sin, the easier it will be for him to forsake his sin.

Restoring Relationships

Sin not only affects our fellowship with God, it also fouls up our relationship with others. Correction is not complete until valid biblical attempts[1] at restoration with all parties are made. Restoration does not necessarily mean that there will be no consequences for one's sin or that the trust which was lost as a result of the transgression will be immediately reinstated. It does mean that those who have knowledge of the sin are made aware that every biblical requirement for correction has been (or is in the process of being) accomplished by the repentant sinner. More importantly, restoration means that the person should be viewed and treated as someone who has repented and has been forgiven.

When the incestuous man in the Corinthian church repented, Paul exhorted the church to "forgive and comfort [him], lest somehow such a one be overwhelmed by excessive sorrow," urging them also to "reaffirm [your] love for him" (2 Cor. 2:7, 8). When the youngest of the two prodigal sons "came to his senses" and returned home, his father threw a celebration to which some of his friends were invited. The celebration included music, dancing, rejoicing, merrymaking, a nice set of clothes for the repentant sinner, and, of course, the best food available (Luke 15:22-32).[2]

Children who sin also need to be restored. They need to be restored to God, to those against whom they have sinned, and to their parents—especially after incidents of corporal punishment. You may be wondering why this is the first mention of corporal punishment in a chapter devoted exclusively to the correction of children. The reason is because the biblical use of the rod is so inextricably woven into the

---

[1] I say *attempts* because, while God is always willing to restore a repentant Christian, sinful man may not be.

[2] Let me emphasize again that the parable doesn't indicate the son did not have to suffer any additional consequences. Apparently, whatever the father had left belonged to the eldest son ("all that is mine is yours," v. 31).

fabric of child training that I've chosen to address it in a separate chapter (Chapter Six: The Rod and Reproof).

Guidelines for Correcting with the Scriptures

1. Identify the specific patterns of sin with which your child is struggling.

We all have our own unique styles of sinning. While it is true there is no temptation that can overtake us "but such as is common to man" (1 Cor. 10:13), it is also true that each of us is tempted when we are carried away and enticed by our *own* desires[1] (James 1:14). Like a large mouth bass being lured by an angler, our desires lure us to sin. The more we give in to those desires, the more we become habituated to sin. Particular sins become increasingly more comfortable for us to commit. We even start to do them unconsciously. If this continues unchecked, we end up in the net like the wretch spoken of in Proverbs 5:22 (NKJV), "His own iniquities entrap the wicked [man], And he is caught in the cords of his sin." Notice that what entraps this man is his "*own* iniquities"—iniquities that were somehow peculiar to him. John

---

[1] We are often blinded to temptation because the sin we are being tempted to commit is something we desire (want) to do. The desire by which we are enticed seems so "natural" to us that we may not recognize it as a temptation to sin. The real culprit is our sinful (wrong or inordinate) desire.

Mason, in his *Treatise on Self Knowledge* published in 1813, discusses what he identifies as one's *constitutional sins.*[1]

> Now, these sins which men are generally most strongly inclined to, and the temptations which they find they have least power to resist, are usually and properly called their constitutional sins...

David also had an awareness of a particular sin into which he was especially prone to fall. "I was also blameless before Him, And I kept myself from *my* iniquity" (Psalm 18:23, NKJV). And the writer of the book of Hebrews speaks of laying aside the sin which *"easily* entangles us" (Heb. 12:1). You may fall into a particular sin more easily than I. I might easily be tempted by something that you could never even imagine doing.

Mason continues:[2]

> Some are more inclined to the sins of the flesh; sensuality, intemperance, uncleanness, sloth, self indulgence, and excess in animal gratifications. Others [are] more inclined to the sins of the spirit; pride, malice, covetousness, ambition, wrath, revenge, envy and the like. And I am persuaded there are a few, but upon a thorough search into themselves, may find that... one of these sins hath ordinarily a greater power over them than the rest....

The process of identifying in biblical terms the particular habitual sins which need to be corrected in your child should technically precede conviction. By rights, this guideline logically belongs in the previous chapter. You must first convict your child of his sinful habit patterns before you can show him how to correct them. I've chosen to address it in this chapter because so often parents try to convict their children of individual sins without identifying the overall patterns of selfishness, pride, fear, anger, rebellion, or whatever else has ensnared their young lives. In so doing, well-meaning parents don't see the for-

---

[1] John Mason, *A Treatise on Self-Knowledge* (London: Thomas Tegg, 1813), p. 49.

[2] Ibid, pp. 50-51.

est through the trees. They spend almost all their time trying to extinguish small fires, all the while ignoring the arsonist who is setting new fires faster than the existing ones can be put out.

It is these patterns of sin in our children's lives that deserve our fullest attention. Now, I'm certainly not suggesting that we ignore those individual sins—those little fires that are more or less unrelated to a pattern. Sin is sin and it cannot be ignored. Of course, sometimes parents may choose to "overlook" or "cover with love" a particular incident of sin in the life of a child (Prov. 19:11, 1 Peter 4:8). Nonhabitual sins do require conviction and to a lesser degree correction. But it is those patterns of sin with which your child continuously struggles where correction is most necessary.

By focusing on the broader pattern, parents can often indirectly help children correct a myriad of other individual sins. For example, helping a child correct an anger problem will at once improve his communication skills, even though little if any time is spent directly teaching him biblical principles of communication. It might also positively affect other areas of his life such as foolishness, friendships, bitterness, depression, and rebellion. So don't be myopic when it comes to dealing with sin. Take a moment to zoom out and see the bigger picture. It may save you a little time and a lot of unnecessary aggravation.

2. Identify those portions of Scripture that specifically address the correction of your child's sin.

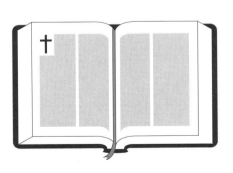

Constitutional Sins

❏ *Anger*
James 4:1
❏ *Selfishness*
Philip. 2:3
❏ *Worry*
Matt. 6:25ff.

By this stage in the process, you've probably gotten some of the work done. To get beyond step two, you must have at least begun the process of locating the Scriptures necessary to convict your child. Now you need to find those that deal with correction. What I suggest you look for are passages addressing the specific things that need to be put off (or forsaken). Sometimes these appear by themselves, and sometimes in lists of other terms which describe various sins. Think also in terms of "who else in Scripture had to face the same or similar circumstance (temptation or sin)?" Pay careful attention to how those individuals handled temptation, confessed and repented of sin, made restitution, and were restored to God and their brothers. Note whether they did it correctly or incorrectly and whether or not God blessed their efforts. You see, it's not enough to show your children where they need to be corrected and teach them how to correct their lives, you also need to explain the biblical basis for doing so.

Let me again refer you to Chapter Seven: *Learning to Use Life's Instruction Manual* (which, in addition to providing practical instructions, also identifies additional resources to help you in your search) and to Appendix A: "Scripture Texts for Child Training" (p. 131), both of which furnish helpful information applicable to all four of the useful purposes of Scripture.

3. Consider the answers to the following questions to help insure you're thoroughly correcting your child.

- Does my child need to change his mind about anything?
- Have I discussed with my child the thoughts and motives of his heart (Heb. 4:12)?
- Has he/she confessed his sin to (and asked forgiveness of) all appropriate parties?
- Is restitution in order?
- Is there anything (people, places, activities, etc.) which must be (at least temporarily) removed from his/her life?
- Is corporal discipline in order (see Chapter Six)?
- Will additional accountability help?
- Does my child understand what God expects him to do next time he/she finds himself/herself in the same or similar circumstance (see Chapter Five)?

Next to the front door of a counseling center where I once had the privilege to work, there hung a hand-painted welcome sign. Underneath the word "Welcome" was an artist's rendering of an open Bible and the words of Psalm 19:7, "The law of the Lord is perfect, restoring the soul." The Hebrew word for "perfect" is *tamiym*. It means complete, whole or entire. This passage is the Old Testament equivalent of 2 Timothy 3:17 where the Scriptures are said to make "perfect" [complete] the man of God and to "thoroughly equip" him for every good work. The Hebrew word used to explain what effect "the law of the Lord" has upon the soul is *shuwb*: to *restore, refresh, or bring back*. Once again, the idea of the Bible's ability to correct some problem that has occurred in the life of the believer is what is being addressed here. The Bible is able to help you correct any (non-organic) behavioral problem in living with which you or your child is struggling. For you to ignore using the Scriptures for this corrective purpose is to not only deny your children enduring help and hope, it is also to deny the God of the Bible, who took thousands of years to provide you with such a tool, and to deny the Holy Spirit indwelling your life to help you understand and apply it. If you've not been using the Word of God as He intended, perhaps the very first thing that needs to be corrected is your own view of the Scriptures. They really are totally sufficient!

Parents must oft whet instruction upon their children: they may not think it enough to tell their children what they ought to do, but to instruction they must add admonition: and, as it were, beat into their children's heads the lessons which they teach them: that so [or *in so doing*] they may make a deeper impression in their hearts. Thus shall their instructions be like the *words of the wise which are as nails flattened* [Ecc. 12:11] or flat knocked in: they remain firm where they are once flattened, and cannot be easily plucked out: for as many blows do knock a nail up to the head (as it were) so many admonitions do settle good instructions in a child's heart, and cause the heart to be established in that which is taught.

William Gouge (1622)[1]

[1] William Gouge, *Of Domestical Duties* (London: William Balden), p. 549. Bound photocopy of this (340-year-old) classic is available through Still Waters Revival Books, 4710 37A Ave., Edmonton AB. Canada, T6L 3T5 (403) 450-3730.

chapter five

Training with the Scriptures

Do you know the difference between teaching and training? The Bible uses a variety of Hebrew and Greek words to distinguish between the two. We will unpack some of those terms in this chapter (and the next) so that you'll be better able to train your children with the Bible after you have taught it to them. Let's begin our look into this matter of distinction with another citation from H. Clay Trumbull's famous work, *Hints on Child Training*.[1]

> The term "training," like the term "teaching," is used in various senses; hence it is liable to be differently understood by different persons, when applied to a single department of a parent's duties in the bringing up of his children. Indeed, the terms "training" and "teaching" are often used interchangeably, as covering the entire process of a child's education. In this sense a child's training is understood to include his teaching; and, again, his teaching is understood to include his training. But in its more restricted sense the training of a child is the shaping, the developing, and the controlling of his personal faculties and powers, while the teaching of a child is the securing to him of knowledge from beyond himself.
>
> It has been said that the essence of teaching is causing another to know. It may similarly be said that the essence of training is causing another to do. Teaching gives knowledge. Training gives skill. Teaching fills the mind.

---

[1] H. Clay Trumbull, *Hints on Child Training*, pp. 1-2. I cited this quotation in Chapter Four of *The Heart of Anger*. Additional material from that chapter has also been integrated into this one. I trust those of you who have read that work will forbear with the overlap and benefit from the fuller explanation and adaptation of the material.

Training shapes the habits. Teaching brings to the child that which he did not have before. Training enables a child to make use of that which is already his possession. We teach a child the meaning of words. We train a child in speaking and walking. We teach him the truths which we have learned for ourselves. We train him in habits of study, that he may be able to learn other truths for himself. Training and teaching must go on together in the wise upbringing of any and every child. The one will fail of its own best end if it be not accompanied by the other. He who knows how to teach a child, is not competent for the oversight of a child's education unless he also knows how to train a child.

Training is a possibility long before teaching is. Before a child is old enough to know what is said to it, it is capable of feeling, and of conforming to, or of resisting, the pressure of efforts for its training. A child can be trained to go to sleep in the arms of its mother or nurse, or in a cradle, or on a bed; with rocking, or without it; in a light room, or in a dark one; in a noisy room, or only in a quiet one; to expect nourishment and to accept it only at fixed hours, or at its own fancy,—while as yet it cannot understand any teaching concerning the importance or the fitness of one of these things. A very young child can be trained to cry for what it wants, or to keep quiet, as means of securing it. And, as a matter of fact, the training of children is begun much earlier than their teaching. Many a child is well started in its life-training by the time it is six weeks old, even though its elementary teaching is not attempted until months after that."

Are you beginning to see the difference between the two? Stay with me. It will become even more apparent.

This fourth and final practical purpose of the Scriptures mentioned in our passage—"training in righteousness"—is, of them all, the most closely associated in the Bible with child training. The Greek word is *paideia*. Perhaps its most famous usage is found in Ephesians 6:4.

> And fathers, do not provoke your children to anger; but bring them up in the discipline and instruction of the Lord.

Here, the word *paideia* has been rendered *discipline*. The word *training*, however, simply is not sufficient to communicate the exact nuance of the original. Neither is it adequate to fully describe the nuance of the original in the passage we have been studying throughout this book. Of course, *paideia* does mean to instruct, to train, or to educate. But there's more to the word than general education. It's a form of education that includes discipline. It's the kind of training that may involve chastisement or the discipline of being made to practice something (like a musical piece or a gymnastic routine) over and over until it is learned.

The Ephesian passage speaks to the two-fold process of biblical parenting: training that involves discipline (*paideia*) and verbal counsel or confrontation (*nouthesia*—which we learned about in Chapter Four).

> This two-sided approach is roughly approximate to what Proverbs 29:15 says about "the rod" and "reproof." Structured discipline (the use of reward and punishment)—i.e., discipline with teeth, discipline that gets the job done—and personal counsel are the two sides of child training which must be kept in balance. Parents frequently err by neglecting one side or the other. The biblical parent will stress both.[1]

We'll unpack Proverbs 29:15 more thoroughly in the next chapter, but for now suffice it to say that if you are not using the Bible when you discipline your children, you are not disciplining them biblically. The goal of this chapter is to help you understand how to practically use the Scriptures for the disciplined training of your children in righteousness.

---

[1] *How to Help People Change*, pp. 169, 170.

Why is training necessary?

"If I have taken my child through the first three steps of the process (teaching, conviction and correction)," you might be wondering, "why bother with the disciplined training in righteousness? After all, if I've made it to step three, my child's problem has been *corrected*."

Yes, for the moment it probably has. But if your child has habituated himself to a particular sin (if he has a pattern or habit of sin—especially what Mason called a "constitutional sin"), correction alone will not work.[1] Remember, we have been talking about progressive sanctification. Our goal is to help our children become Christ-like, not merely to help them stop living like the devil. It is to make them wise, not just to undo their foolishness. In the last chapter, I pointed out that the third step in our process (correction) corresponds to the concept of putting off sin, whereas the fourth step (disciplined training in righteousness) corresponds to the idea of putting on righteousness. In that chapter, I developed the "put-off" side; here I'll elaborate further on the "put-on" side.

According to our text, the Scriptures are useful for "disciplined training *in righteousness*." Righteousness is the goal of your child training—the righteousness of Christ. The Scriptures are able to give your child "the wisdom that leads to salvation through faith which is in Christ Jesus." Initially, they are able to help him see his need to accept by faith (in His atoning sacrifice) the imputation of Christ's perfect righteousness to his account. "He [*God*] made Him [*Christ*] who knew no sin [to be] sin on our behalf, that we might become the righteousness of God in Him" (2 Cor. 5:21). Then, when he has been regenerated (and the law books in heaven have been adjusted to show that your child has been credited legally with the righteousness of Christ), the Scriptures are able to train him to increasingly manifest Christ's righteousness practically and tangibly in his life.[2] The first kind of righteousness is that of *justification* which comes by faith instantaneously the moment a person believes the gospel (Acts 13:38, 39;

---

[1] Disciplined training in righteousness is helpful, even if the sin you have corrected is not habitual, in that it will increase the likelihood the sin will occur less frequently (if at all) in the future.

[2] The pattern of many of the New Testament epistles reflects this truth. They

Rom. 5). The second kind is the righteousness of *sanctification* which comes gradually as a person is led by the Holy Spirit, Who produces His special fruit (in its season) through (by means of) the Word of God (cf. Gal. 5:18-23; 2 Cor. 3:17, 18). It is this second kind of righteousness in which we all, as believers in Jesus Christ, must be trained.

Neither kind of righteousness is our own. Both come from God. Both require God's Spirit and God's Word to produce. One (the first) is an act of God. The other is at once an act of God and a process that requires our active cooperation. Of course, although sanctification requires your cooperation, it is not your doing. "It is God Who is producing in you both the willingness and the ability to do the things that please Him" (Phil. 2:13, CCNT). And even though you must participate in the process, ultimately its success is not dependent on you. No one is more committed to your sanctification (and that of your believing child) than God. As David so aptly put it, "The Lord *will* perfect [that] [which] concerns me" (Psalm 138:8). And He will continue to perfect us until the day we die or the day He returns (whichever comes first).

The Gumnazo Principle

Before we go on to some practical considerations, there is another very important New Testament word I'd like to unpack for you. In *The Heart of Anger*, I wrote about something called the *gumnazo* principle.[1] *Gumnazo* is another New Testament word for "training."

> When I was growing up on Long Island, I was given as one of my chores the daily responsibility of sweeping the kitchen floor after supper. I was made to do this task *whether or not I felt like it*. I did it repeatedly and regularly day in and day out for many years. I never really enjoyed sweeping but went from hating it to tolerating it. I continued sweeping year after year until I went to col-

---

begin with doctrine which deals in one way or another with the legal elements of justification (being declared righteous) and end up with various exhortations to live out (or live up to) that righteousness in daily living.

[1] *The Heart of Anger*, pp. 61-64.

lege. Finally I was liberated from the bondage of the broom.

Seven years ago when I first came to Atlanta, I was preparing lunch in the church basement kitchen which was graciously loaned to me for my first counseling office. Opening the pantry door, I discovered a pile of sugar in the middle of the closet floor. What do you suppose my next conscious thought was? If you are thinking, "Sweep it up!" you are wrong. My next conscious thought came after I had walked out the kitchen door, down a long hallway, entered a utility closet, located a broom, left the closet, and was walking down the hall again on my way back to the kitchen with the broom in my hand. My next conscious thought was, "Lou, what are you doing? Nobody asked you to sweep the floor. No one is going to give you Brownie points for sweeping the floor. You are sweeping the floor because it is the *right* thing to do."

The years I spent sweeping the kitchen floor as a youth, as well as the subsequent discipline I had gone through, had been used by God to develop a good habit. A habit is something that is practiced so frequently it becomes second nature. It is a routine that has become so natural it can be accomplished quickly, easily, automatically, and (as in my case) unconsciously. Over the years, I had disciplined myself for the purpose of sweeping a messy floor. Paul told Timothy to discipline himself for the purpose of godliness. "But discipline yourself for the purpose of godliness" (1 Timothy 4:7). The word discipline (*gumnazo*—from which we get such words as gymnastics and gymnasium) means to exercise or to train. The idea is that of a man who decides to begin training with weights to increase his strength. The first day at the gym he attempts to press 80 pounds, but finds that he cannot lift the barbell above his head. Consequently, he decides to start with 50 pounds. He discovers that he can press the 50 pound barbell 12 times over his head. He then continues to exercise with this weight for one week. The next week he increases the barbell weight to 60 pounds. He maintains the 60 pound weight for seven days then graduates to 70 pounds. All the while his muscles get stronger and larger. Week by week he continues increasing the weight until after two years he is easily pressing over 175 pounds. On his two-year weight-lifting anniversary, he walks over to the 80 pound barbell that he could not lift above his knees on his first day of training. With one hand, he lifts that weight all the way over his head. His muscles have become so strong and so large that what was once impossible has become easy because of training and exercise (*gumnazo*). This is exactly what happens when we exercise ourselves for the purpose of godliness. What once seemed impossible becomes easy (second nature).

Now what does all this have to do with children? Consider the following two verses and keep in mind the meaning of *gumnazo* as you read.

"For everyone who partakes [only] of milk is not accustomed to the word of righteousness, for he is a babe. But solid food is for the mature, who because of practice have their senses trained [*gumnazo*ed] to discern good and evil" (Hebrews 5:13-14).

The context of these two verses is a rebuke. Some of the Hebrew Christians who had not developed to the point of being teachers as they should have (in light of the time they had been given to grow into mature Christians) are being rebuked. The biblical author uses developmental language to contrast the growth and training of children to the growth and training of Christians. He assumes that the reader understands an essential universal principle of child development that our culture seems to have forgotten—training. Two words in particular are employed to communicate this principle. I like to refer to it as the "Gumnazo Principle." The word *gumnazo* is used again in this verse as it is used in I Timothy 4:7. Again its meaning "to train by exercise" can be clearly seen in this passage. The second word, which actually appears first in this text, is the word *exis,* which means a habit or a practice that has been produced by continual past exercise so that it has become a "second nature."

Next, let's consider Hebrews 12:7-11. In this passage, the Holy Spirit repeatedly uses forms of the word *paideia* to speak of the discipline God the Father employs in the process of spanking every true child of His. Then, He uses the word *gumnazo* to summarize the *training* which has been accomplished by the chastisement. In other words, *gumnazo* (training by exercise or practice) and *paideia* (training with discipline) are used rather synonymously.

> It is for discipline (*paideia*) that you endure; God deals with you as with sons; for what son is there whom his father does not discipline (*paideuo*)? But if you are without discipline (*paideia*), of which all have become partakers, then you are illegitimate children and not sons. Furthermore, we had earthly fathers to discipline (*paideutês: a person who chastens*) us, and we respected them; shall we not much rather be subject to the Father of spirits, and live? For they disciplined (*paideuo*) us for a short time as seemed best to them, but He disciplines us for our good, that we may share His holiness. All discipline (*paideia*) for the moment seems not to be joyful, but sorrowful; yet to those who have been *trained* (*gumnazo*) by it, afterwards it yields the peaceful fruit of righteousness.

Again we see the purpose for which training is endured is experiential *righteousness.* The Holy Spirit produces fruit in our life that, when eaten, tastes like peace. Allow me to continue my observations about this passage by once more citing from *The Heart of Anger.*[1] As you read, take note of how closely the Gumnazo Principle corresponds to the "put-on" side of the two-fold process of change.

---

[1] *The Heart of Anger,* pp.64-66.

The context here is "how to handle a spanking from God." The author is exhorting his readers to endure chastening from the Lord, knowing that it will produce the "peaceable fruits of righteousness to those who have been exercised (*gumnazo*) by it" (KJV). As we saw before, a contrast is made between how children respond to chastening by their fathers and how Christians are to respond to chastening by their Heavenly Father. Again the author assumes some knowledge of that essential principle of child training I have referred to as "the Gumnazo Principle."

The Gumnazo Principle can be illustrated by the example of a blacksmith who is training an apprentice. Apprenticeships are not as popular today as they were during the early days of our nation when Benjamin Franklin, for example, served as an apprentice under his older brother. Then it was not uncommon for the apprentice to live with, be provided for, and be subject to the master craftsman. An apprenticeship was a thorough, intense training that usually lasted for seven years. Basically, it was training by practice, practice and more practice, until the apprentice got it right. The master craftsman would first explain and demonstrate the equipment. Then he would likely allow the apprentice to observe him going through the entire process of making a horseshoe, from lighting the billows to shoeing the horse's hoof with the finished product, explaining each procedure in great detail. After a number of observations, the master craftsman would allow the apprentice to help with some of the procedure. Instructing him, the master would allow the apprentice to try the procedure. He would correct him on the spot should he make a mistake and *require him to do it again* until he got it right. The master may have stood behind his apprentice, holding or gripping his hands over the hands of the apprentice as they would hold the iron in the fire until it had just the right glow of red. Then, *hand in hand,* the master craftsman and the apprentice would quickly bring the iron to the anvil, and, *hand in hand,* the master would demonstrate to the apprentice just where to hammer the iron and just how hard to strike it. Then he would put it back into the fire and so on until the horseshoe was complete. After a few exercises of this hands-on training, the master would be ready to allow the apprentice to try the procedure by himself. Still standing behind his student, he would observe the apprentice's work, noticing every detail of workmanship. Then as soon as a mistake was made, *immediately* he would say, "No, this way." Again grasping the hand of the apprentice, he would show him precisely how to correct his mistake. That's "the Gumnazo Principle" in action!

Imagine what it would have been like if the master craftsman had simply explained the procedure one time and when the apprentice made his first mistake, the master said, "Wrong! No dinner for you tonight. You'd better improve tomorrow."

"That would be cruel, unmerciful, and a violation of education," you say.

Yet that is the way many Christian parents "discipline" their children. "That was disrespectful!" they say, as they cruelly slap the child across the face with the backside of a hand, while feeling good about the fact that they identified exactly what the child did wrong—being disrespectful.

The Gumnazo Principle maintains that you haven't disciplined a child properly until you have brought him to the point of repentance by requiring him to practice the biblical alternative to sinful behavior. This would involve not just asking forgiveness for the disrespect and not just identifying the sin by name (two essential steps in biblical discipline), but also would involve responding with a respectful alternative to the disrespect using the appropriate words, tone of voice and non-verbal communication.

Imagine what it would be like trying to teach your son how to tie a double Windsor in his necktie or trying to teach your daughter how to make and roll out a pie crust without "the Gumnazo Principle." At some point, unless you have unlimited time and resources, you would have to stop the process of verbal instruction and show your child how to correct a mistake. If the Gumnazo Principle is vital for teaching such relatively simple and temporal tasks, how much more is it necessary for teaching the application of eternal truth and the development of Christ-like character.

Developing Habits

What comes to mind when you hear the word *habits*? For many this word has negative connotations. Perhaps this is because before a person comes to Christ, the habits he develops are usually bad ones. Our sin nature and our flesh naturally predispose us to a kind of *training* that is immoral. In fact, the word *gumnazo* is used in the Bible not only for the godly kind of training but also for the ungodly. Peter, speaking of certain ungodly individuals who were somehow mingling with the true believers to whom he was writing, uses *gumnazo* to describe the development of a particular wrong habit.

> They are stains and blemishes, reveling in their deceptions, as they carouse with you, having eyes full of adultery and that never cease from sin, enticing unstable souls, having a heart *trained* [*gumnazo*ed] in greed, accursed children; forsaking the right way they have gone astray, having followed the way of Balaam, the [son] of Beor, who loved the wages of unrighteousness.
>
> (2 Peter 2:13-15)

Also, the Hebrew scholars who translated the Septuagint (the Greek version of the Old Testament from which Jesus frequently quoted) used *gumnazo* to express the same kind of sinful habituation.

> Can the Ethiopian change his skin or the leopard its spots? Neither can you do good who are *accustomed* to doing evil. (Jer. 13:23, NIV)

Your children have this bent toward developing sinful habits. Apart from Christ and His Word, they will habituate themselves to speak, act, think and be motivated in ways that are displeasing to God. Left to their own devices, they will be filled with their own ways (cf. Prov. 1:30, 31; 14:14). They will also cause you much pain: "A child left to himself disgraces his mother" (Prov. 29:15, NIV). But with the help of the Spirit and the Scriptures, you can (and must) train your children to think, speak, act, and be motivated biblically.

Now, if you don't already do so, I'd like to invite you to think of habits in a more positive light. The ability to form habits is truly a blessing from God for which we ought to be thankful. Habits enable us to do things comfortably, automatically, skillfully, and unconsciously.[1] Think of how complicated life would be without the ability to develop habits. Ladies, imagine what it would be like if you had to put on your makeup every day without the aid of habit. Every day you would likely spend hours trying to put on your face. You'd first have to rummage through the vanity to collect just the right cosmetics from the entire collection. Next, you'd have to figure out how to open and close all manner of jars, bottles, tubes, and those other unusually-shaped containers, the function of which we men can only speculate. You would have to relearn (every day) how to skillfully apply all that stuff with a dozen varieties of those funny-looking applicators. Then you would have to experiment with learning to apply the exact amount, in the exact shade, in the exact places to give you the exact look you want. You would doubtless want to try at least two or three different styles (like many of you do every day with your clothing) before you're satisfied with the results. You wouldn't get to breakfast by midnight! But now, because of habit, you can perform this rather complex behavior (this creative work of art) automatically, skillfully, and unconsciously. And you can do it *while* talking on the phone, watching the morning news, giving instructions to your children, getting instructions from your husband, or (like too many women I've known) driving your car (*please don't do that!*).

And you fellows, what if you couldn't remember how to tie that necktie, or operate that car, or drive that golf ball, or cast that fly, or

---

[1] *How to Help People Change*, p. 193.

fire that rifle, or shoot that basketball or worse—what if you forgot how to use the remote control!? How much desire would you have to do those things if they always required the exertion of tremendous effort? Do you see how much you have been blessed because of your habits?

Thankfully we do have the ability to develop habits. Sadly, indwelling sin makes it easy to develop bad habits. But your job as a parent is to train your children to develop good habits.[1] Good habits are what character is all about. The more a person exercises himself for the purpose of godliness, the more godly he becomes. The more godly (like Christ) he becomes, the more he acquires the character of Christ. This, you remember, (from Chapter One) is the goal of biblical parenting. But it cannot be accomplished apart from using the Scriptures. "Disciplined training in righteousness," therefore, is essential to the process of Christian character.

Practical Considerations

Now that you have a better understanding of what it means to train your children in righteousness, we must consider how to use the Scriptures practically for this purpose.

1. Start your children on a regular program of Scripture memory.

There is simply nothing more effective to help you train your children in righteousness than this! The more of God's Word your children have internalized, the more God's Spirit will have to work with as He sanctifies them. One can hardly imagine a better way for a parent to cooperate with the Spirit's work in the life of his child than to give Him His most important weapon: "the sword of the Spirit, which is the

---

[1] Let me plainly state that by using the phrase "develop good habits," I'm not referring to some sort of behavior modification technique, but rather to the process and goal of sanctification which is produced by the Holy Spirit in conjunction with the Word of God. The change of habits I speak of are not just superficial external behaviors, such as words and actions, but penetrate to the habits of the heart: one's thoughts and motives (cf. Heb. 4:12).

Word of God" (Eph. 6:17). The word for "word" in this passage is not the term that usually appears in the phrase Word of God elsewhere in Scripture. Usually the Greek word *logos* (the written word) is used. Here the word *rhema* (the spoken word) is used. It is the Word of God that has been internalized, is spoken in one's heart, and is ready on one's lips that the Spirit most efficaciously uses in His sanctifying work. Remember what Deuteronomy 6:6 says to you Mom and Dad, "And these words, which I am commanding you today, shall be on *your heart*." After you have internalized them, you are to impress them deeply (or whet them) upon your children's hearts.

Scripture memory helps train children in righteousness in several ways. Firstly, it is effective in correcting existing problems (it helps in putting off sin). Secondly, it assists in the development of new habits (the put-on process) and thirdly, it helps prevent new problems from developing in the future.

Do you want your kids to know and do God's will? Let them do what the psalmists did.

> I delight to do Thy will, O my God;
> Thy Law is within my heart.   (Ps. 40:8)

> Thy word I have treasured in my heart,
> That I may not sin against Thee.   (Ps. 119:11)

"But my children can't memorize!"

"Really!" Have they memorized their names? Do they know where they live? Have they committed your telephone number to memory? How about the phone numbers of their friends? Do they know how old they are and when their birthdays are? Do they remember what kind of goodies they like as they accompany you down their favorite aisle in the supermarket? Do they have any difficulty remembering the medicines they don't enjoy taking? You see, memorization is not simply a matter of IQ; rather it is a matter of DQ (Desire Quotient). For most of us, our child's ability to memorize is not primarily a function of his intelligence, but of his will. It is a matter of what he values, loves and believes necessary for life and happiness.

Jesus said in Matthew 4:4. "Man shall not live on bread alone, but on every word that proceeds out of the mouth of God." Let me ask you something. Would your kids be better able to memorize Scripture if I promised to give them $250 for every chapter they internalized? Would you be more motivated by such an offer? According to the Bible, that would be a small reward for your efforts. "The law of Thy mouth is better to me than thousands of gold and silver [pieces]" (Psalm 119:72).

"But," you say, "my kids have no desire to memorize Scripture. You can lead a horse to water but you can't make him drink." Oh yes you can—if you put enough salt in his oats! You may be better able to inculcate a desire for God's word in your children than you realize. Milieu teaching is the key. As your children see the truth of Matthew 4:4 ("Man shall not live on bread alone, but on every word that proceeds out of the mouth of God") consistently lived out in your life, they may soon realize why the early Christians were called followers of the way: because biblical Christianity is the best way to interpret life and the only way of life that truly makes sense! Until your little ponies catch your enthusiasm for the Scriptures, there is another way you can "make them drink." When my older daughter says to me, "Daddy I don't like (or want to do) something," I routinely reply, "That's OK honey. You don't have to like (or want to do) it. You just have to eat (or do) it." She doesn't always *want to* memorize her Bible verses, but Kim and I are training her to do it *whether or not she feels like it!* She has memorized many passages when she would rather have been doing other things. And as I told you at the beginning, she has learned them well enough to use them effectively.

Do you remember the list of your child's constitutional sins and the list of corresponding Scriptures I suggested you develop at the end of the last chapter? Why not begin encouraging your child to memorize some of the passages on that list?

Constitutional Sins

❑ *Anger*
James 4:1
❑ *Selfishness*
Philip. 2:3
❑ *Worry*
Matt. 6:25ff.

Remember, this is a spiritual *discipline*. And the greatest enemy to discipline is your feelings. Keep in mind also that when a person memorizes just one verse of Scripture, he memorizes one element of God's thinking. But when he internalizes an entire paragraph or chapter of the Bible, he memorizes God's *thought patterns*.

2. Train your children to meditate on Scripture.

Another powerful means of disciplined training in righteousness is to train your children (especially your older children) in the discipline of biblical meditation. Meditation fastens into our hearts truths which we received but have not yet assimilated into our character. Meditation is a means the Spirit of God effectively uses to permanently amalgamate into our character that *truth* which previously we may have only received intellectually or superficially—truth that had not yet been digested and become a part of our makeup. In 1666, a Puritan preacher published a book entitled *Heart Treasure* which had much to say about biblical meditation. I've taken the liberty to update into modern English a small section of this fine work. [1]

> Christian meditation is the contemplative and earnest fixing of the mind on the great spiritual realities which the Bible has revealed to us.... Meditation is the soul's conference with itself; the discourse which it holds with truth obtained, and impressions received, in the secret sanctuary of its own consciousness. It is the... solemn endeavor of the soul to bring home to itself divine things, and so to resolve, ponder, and digest them, as to work their transforming power into every element and faculty of its being.... It is the digestive process by which spiritual food nourishes the soul and promotes its growth in holiness.
>
> Lack of meditation is the primary reason that so many professing Christians, in spite of exposure to the most excellent teaching, still remain ignorant, unstable, and

---

[1] Oliver Heywood, *Heart Treasure* (Beaver Falls, PA: Soli Deo Gloria, 1666), pp. 250ff.

unfruitful, "ever learning, but never able to come to the knowledge of the truth." Instruction flows in upon them from all sides; but their hearts and minds are like sieves, out of which everything runs as fast as it is poured in. The impressions which truth makes on their minds are as temporary as characters traced on the sands of the seashore, which the next wave erases forever. But meditation *imprints truth deeply* on the conscience, and *engraves* it on the tablets of the inner man, as with the point of a diamond or a laser beam. It thus becomes incorporated into the soul; and forms, as it were, a part of it; and it is ever present, to regulate the heart's affections and to control and guide all of its movements.

As to the definition of biblical meditation, no one has said it more succinctly than J. I. Packer.

Meditation is the activity of calling to mind, and thinking over and dwelling on, and applying to oneself, the various things that one knows about the works and ways and purposes of God. [1]

In his book *The Christian's Daily Walk in Holy Security and Peace,* Mr. Scudder addresses the issue of biblical meditation.[2] Here again I have updated the Old English vernacular.

Merely reading, hearing, and having transient thoughts of biblical truths do not leave *half* that impression of goodness upon the soul, which they would do, if they might be recalled, and fixed there by *serious* thought. Without this meditation, the good food of the soul passes through the understanding, and therein is quite lost. It is like *raw* and *undigested food*, which does not nourish those creatures that chew the cud until they have retrieved it back and

---

[1] J. I. Packer, *Knowing God* (Downers Grove, IL: Intervarsity Press, 1973), p. 23.
[2] Henry Scudder, *The Christian's Daily Walk in Holy Security and Peace* (reprinted edition; Harrisonburg, VA: Sprinkle Publications), p. 108.

chewed it better. Meditation is the Christian's way of chewing the cud. All the outward means of salvation do little good in comparison, except that by meditation they are thoroughly considered, and laid up in the heart.... Meditation digests, engrafts, and turns the spiritual knowledge gained from God's Word...into the very life and substance of the soul, changing and transforming you according to it, so that God's will as revealed in the Bible and your will become one, so that you choose and delight in the same things as He does.

It is beyond the scope of this book to delve into the many specifics of how to meditate on Scripture. It will have to suffice to encourage you to do your own research into the subject. Sound Word Associates carries my cassette tape (#LP56) with the accompanying handout entitled *How to Meditate on Scripture,* which will provide much more detailed practical assistance than I can provide in this little book. Also, Appendix C: "Projects in Proverbs" (p. 145) is a practical Bible-study method that facilitates memorizing the Proverbs, which older children and teenagers may find enjoyable. It can be done individually or as a "family time" study.

3. When employing the Gumnazo Principle, be sure to reference the appropriate Scripture passages.

Although the process of sanctification modifies behavior, it is not the same thing as behavior modification. Those who assert that biblical parenting is little more than Scripture-coated behavior modification make the same fundamental error that was made by some of Christ's critics (the Sadducees). They understood neither the Scriptures nor the power of God (cf. Matt. 22:23-33). Both parent and child must depend upon both the Spirit and the Word to produce the desired change. To do otherwise is to produce a little Pharisee.

Explaining to children the Biblical directives to put on specific patterns of thought or behavior helps them to realize that it is God Himself (not you) who is requiring the change. It also can serve to remind them that their motive for changing should be to please Him. (Of course, this motive is something you should regularly refer to in the milieu.) Here are a few suggestions to help you incorporate the Scriptures with your child.

- Take him to the passages that tell him what to put off and put on.
- Tell him how you have applied those passages in your own life.
- Help him find creative ways to personally implement the passage.

4. Train your children to obey your instructions.

Perhaps the chief characteristic of the wise son spoken of in the book of Proverbs is that he "heeds his father's instruction" (Prov. 13:1, NKJV; cf. 1:8; 9:9, 19:20). On the other hand, the chief characteristic of the foolish son is that he "rejects his father's instruction" (Prov. 15:5, NKJV; cf. 1:7; 5:12, 23). These passages underscore our prime objective of biblical parenting: producing wise children. Moreover the New Testament, speaking directly to sons and daughters, commands, "Children, obey your parents in the Lord, for this is right" (Eph. 6:1). Then, citing the first of the Ten Commandments which has a promise attached to it (Exod. 20:12), the Holy Spirit again addresses children directly: "Honor your father and mother." It's your responsibility to teach your children passages such as these, to convict and correct them when they violate these passages, and to train them in righteousness so that they will be more obedient in the future.

The Greek verb *to obey* in Ephesians 6:1 means "to heed" or "listen with the intent of doing" that which has been commanded. As John MacArthur points out in his excellent book *Successful Christian Parenting,* the command to honor one's father and mother also implies obedience.[1]

> Scripture repeatedly underscores and expands the Fifth Commandment principle, teaching us that honoring our parents involves obeying them (Deuteronomy 21:18-20; Ephesians 6:1); honoring them with our words (Exodus

---

[1] John MacArthur, *Successful Christian Parenting* (Nashville, TN: Word Publishing, 1999), pp. 108, 109. While married children are always to respect their parents, they are no longer obligated to obey them since, by virtue of the marriage covenant, they have left their parents (Genesis 2:24) to establish a new decision-making unit for Christ.

21:17; Leviticus 20:9; Proverbs 20:20; 30:11); showing them respect in every way (Leviticus 19:3), even with our facial expressions (Proverbs 30:17); hearkening to their counsel (Proverbs 23:22-25); and not treating them lightly in any sense (Deuteronomy 27:16; Ezekiel 22:7).

Children should also be trained to obey the first time they are instructed. In the final analysis, delayed obedience is disobedience. Although there is a time and place for making appeals, when you routinely allow your children to not obey the first time they are given directives, you are training them to procrastinate.

Scripture is "useful" for the process of training children to obey. How familiar are your children with the Scripture passages that speak of their responsibility to obey? How often do you show your children from the Bible exactly what command or principle they are violating? How often do you explain to them from the Bible exactly what they are to put off in terms of disobedience and put on (in its place)?

5. Train your children to communicate biblically.

Communication involves more than just finding and using the right words (cf. Prov. 16:24). It also involves selecting an appropriate tone of voice (cf. Prov. 16:21) and non-verbal forms of communication (cf. Acts 12:17). If you are going to train your children how to communicate biblically, you must learn how to *gumnazo* them in all three areas.

In chapter five of *The Heart of Anger*, I have shown in detail how to apply the Gumnazo Principle to training children in biblical communication principles. Rather than duplicate that material in its entirety here, I will simply refer you to that chapter.

6. Train your children to think biblically.

The ability to shape children's thoughts and motives is something very few parents (even believing parents) seriously consider. However, since the Word of God is the "discerner of the thoughts and intents (motives) of the heart" (Heb. 4:12), the Bible is very useful for training children to develop biblical thought patterns and motivations. In fact, such training cannot truly be done apart from the Scriptures. You see, it is not enough for you to train your children to behave like Christians. You must also train them to think and be motivated in Christ-like ways.[1]

In chapters 7 and 8 of *The Heart of Anger*, I've detailed a biblical approach[2] to drawing out, diagnosing, and correcting unbiblical thoughts and motives which I'll not entirely replicate here. One of the most important things to remember about training your child to think biblically is what Jesus said in Luke 6:45 about the mouth revealing (and sometimes betraying) that which is in the heart. "The good man out of the good treasure of his heart brings forth what is good; and the evil [man] out of the evil [treasure] brings forth what is evil; for his mouth speaks from that which fills his heart." You may not judge what your child's thoughts and motives are, but you may get a glimpse of what is gong on by listening to what he says.[3]

> Although Scripture forbids us from judging what is in the heart of another (I Cor. 4:5; James 2:4), we are permitted to ask him to judge his own thoughts and motives (Acts

---

[1] For information on the distinctives of biblical thinking see my cassette tape *Do You Think Like a Christian,* available through Sound Word Associates.

[2] There are doubtless other (and better) approaches that could be employed by a parent to train a child to think and be motivated like a Christian than the one I've outlined in *The Heart of Anger*. The verbal or written use of a Heart Journal is one of many approaches to getting the job done.

[3] *The Heart of Anger*, pp. 94.

5:1-4; 1 Cor. 11:28-31; 2 Cor. 13:5). Consider Proverbs 20:5, "Counsel in the *heart* of man is deep water; but a man of understanding will *draw* it out." (KJV)

As parents, you can draw out of your child's heart the necessary data to help him biblically diagnose any sin problem that resides therein by learning how to ask specific questions. To the extent that you can draw the counsel out of your heart, you will be able to help him change not only his words, actions and attitudes, but also (and more importantly) his thoughts and motives. And this (forgive the pun) is the "heart of the matter" when it comes to helping anyone change. To the extent that you are not able to draw out the thoughts and motives of his heart, your ability to help him change at the deepest level (the only kind of change that pleases God) will be hindered. Of course, to make an accurate diagnosis of your child's thoughts and motives, the Scripture must be employed as the diagnostic tool....

The only divinely-approved diagnostic manual whereby Christians may accurately judge thoughts and motives is Scripture. Christian parent, you must learn how to not only draw the thoughts and motives out of your child, but also how to diagnose those thoughts and motives "not in words taught by human wisdom [i.e., defense mechanism, reaction formation, love hunger, co-dependency, etc.] but in those taught by the Spirit [i.e., pride, blame-shifting, idolatry, bondage, etc.], combining (interpreting) spiritual thoughts with spiritual words." (I Cor. 2:13)

When you hear your child say things that are inconsistent with Scripture, do you show him from the Bible what is wrong with what he said? When your child does something wrong, do you talk to him about what is going through his mind? When he displays some sinful attitude, do you try to help him figure out what he is wanting, craving, or lusting after that might be generating his bad attitude? Do you show him from Scripture alternative ways to think? Do you pray with him about developing purer motives and talk to him about how he might cultivate more God-glorifying desires? If you answered "no" to any of these questions, you're simply not utilizing the Scriptures as effectively as you could be in your child training. May God grant you the wisdom, patience and self-discipline to effectively use the Bible for the "disciplined training in righteousness" of all your children.

There is instruction which is accommo-
dated to their [children's] rational powers and
correction which is to be applied to their
senses; and here great prudence is to be used.
Correction is never to be administered without
instruction; for then it will likely lose its
impact. Hence, the *Hebrew* and *Greek* languages have one and the same word for both,
both being designed for reformation. Correction is not ordinarily to be used when conviction by reproof will as well obtain the goal.

Samuel Willard[1]

Biblical discipline is *correction*, and that
means that the pattern of the child's behavior
must be changed by instruction in righteousness. He must be shown the error of his way,
and then directed to the proper path. This
requires explanation and instruction. Biblical
discipline demands words.

Bruce A. Ray[2]

---

[1] *Duties of Parents* (Fire and Ice), p. 604.
[2] *Withhold Not Correction* (Phillipsburg, NJ: Presbyterian and Reformed Publishing Company), p. 87.

chapter six

The Rod and Reproof

Let me begin this chapter by again suggesting that if you, like so many Christian parents I've known, are spanking your children without also (simultaneously) ministering the Word to them, you are not spanking them biblically. You see, corporal punishment (the rod) was never intended to be the principal means of correcting your children—at least not by itself. "The rod *and reproof* give wisdom, but a child who gets his own way brings shame to his mother" (Prov. 29:15). Spanking was not designed to be routinely used to discipline children apart from verbal Scriptural confrontation.

Spanking alone simply isn't enough! The rod must be accompanied by verbal confrontation and instruction in order for it to be effective. Can you imagine how you would respond after being pulled to the side of the road by a policeman and then carried off to jail having never been spoken to by the arresting officer? How you would feel if, at your first court appearance, you were fined $750 and sentenced to six months in prison by a judge who never said a word to you but simply wrote his verdict on a card and handed it to the bailiff to carry out the sentence? Imagine how frustrating it would be as you sat in prison, not knowing what laws you had violated or for how long you would have to be incarcerated. You'd probably be more angry at the system for robbing you of justice than you would be grieved over your own alleged transgression of the law. The same principle holds true for your children. You must verbally teach, convict, correct and train your children and do so with the Scriptures when you find it necessary to chastise them. To do otherwise is to provoke them to anger.

When those I counsel do not obey the Bible, I don't spank them. Instead, I must rely on teaching, conviction, correction, and instruction in righteousness. You'll not be able to spank your children indefinitely. Someday, when they are grown, you will have to rely solely on the Bible to impact your children—you'll have to treat them as adults.[1]

---

[1] In the Hebrew culture children were considered to be full adults when they

But until then both the rod and reproof will be necessary. Consider the following diagram:

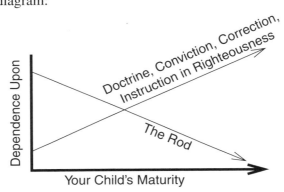

Ideally, as your child matures, the use of corporal discipline should diminish as you seek to correct his behavior, while the use of the Scriptures should increase until your child is so wise that he responds entirely to reproof. "A rebuke goes deeper into one who has understanding than a hundred blows into a fool" (Prov. 17:10). The more you train (*gumnazo*) your children to respond wisely to biblical teaching, reproof, and instruction when you have the aid of the rod, the more likely they will respond wisely to the Scriptures when they are too old for you to spank.

Responding to Reproof

"But," you may ask, "what does a wise response to reproof look

---

were somewhere between 11 and 13 years old. The bar (bas) mitzvah celebrated this event. Without wanting to impose on my readers that which cannot be argued from Scripture alone, let me suggest that children be taught early and in the milieu so that hopefully somewhere between ages 11 and 13 and depending on their maturity, spanking will cease. The quicker the child responds to doctrine, conviction, correction, and disciplined training in righteousness, the sooner corporal punishment may cease. It is interesting to note that fools will always (even when they are adults) require some kind of physical punishment to get their attention, and even then there is no guarantee they will change. "A whip is for the horse, a bridle for the donkey, And a rod for the back of fools" (Prov. 26:3; see also 7:22, 17:10, 18:6, 27:22).

like?" Let me begin my answer by showing you from the Bible what a wrong response looks like. The book of Proverbs provides at least three foolish reactions to reproof. The *first* is to spurn reproof. Wisdom personified, warning about the consequences of not listening to her reproof, says (Prov. 1:30), "They would not accept my counsel, They *spurned* all my reproof." The word for spurn means "to despise" or "to treat with contempt." Some foolish children not only despise reproof, they also despise the reprover (cf. Prov. 9:8, 15:12).

Another sinful response to reproof is to *forsake* it. "He is [on] the path of life who heeds instruction, But he who forsakes reproof goes astray" (Prov. 10:17). You will remember that this word "forsake" (*azab*), which we looked at in Chapter Four, means to leave or abandon (Proverbs 28:13, "He who conceals his transgressions will not prosper, but he who confesses and *forsakes* [them] will find compassion"). The general attitude of someone who has forsaken reproof is typically that of prideful rejection: "I don't want to have anything to do with being corrected anymore."

The *third* foolish response to being reproved in the book of Proverbs is found in verse 10 of Chapter 15. "Stern discipline is for him who forsakes the way; he who *hates* reproof will die." According to one Hebrew scholar, the verb *to hate*

> ...expresses an emotional attitude towards persons and things which are opposed, detested, despised and with which one wishes to have no contact or relationship. The hated and hating person are considered foes or enemies and are considered odious and utterly unappealing.[1]

This proverb says the child who hates reproof "will die" (be destroyed). Another proverb (12:1) exclaims the insensibility of the one who hates reproof: "Whoever loves discipline loves knowledge, but he who *hates* reproof is stupid (as dumb as an ox)." The more your child manifests these foolish responses to reproof, the more necessary it may be for you to rely on the rod to drive such foolishness from him.

---

[1] R. Laird Harris, *Theological Wordbook of the Old Testament*, Volume 2, (Chicago: Moody Press, 1980), p. 880.

Now on the other hand, the book of Proverbs gives just as vivid a picture of the wise person who responds correctly to reproof. In like manner, we'll look at three snapshots of this individual. Wisdom personified again begins by imploring (in 1:23), "*Turn* to my reproof, behold, I will pour out my spirit on you; I will make my words known to you." The word translated "turn" is the foremost Old Testament term for "repent." It involves the same concept we looked at earlier in our discussion of repentance: the idea of turning away from evil and turning toward good. A wise man not only turns away from the sin for which he is being reproved, he also turns favorably towards the one who reproves him, and like David says,

> Let the righteous strike me;
> [It shall be] a kindness.
> And let him rebuke me;
> [It shall be] as excellent oil;
> Let my head not refuse it.   (Psalm 141:5, NKJV)

The *second* proper response is to *regard* reproof. "Poverty and shame [will come] to him who neglects discipline, But he who *regards* reproof will be honored" (Prov. 13:18). To regard something is to "exercise great care over" (or pay careful attention to) it.[1] The word may also be translated to "wait upon" or "attend to" someone or something. The clear idea then is that a wise man (or child) will carefully consider both the charges made against him and any advice about correcting the problem in his life for which he is being reproved. He will not react with defensive pride or dismiss the charges without thorough deliberation.

The *third* appropriate response to reproof is *listening* (or hearing). "He whose ear *listens* to the life-giving reproof will dwell among the wise" (Prov. 15:31). The word denotes more than the mere ability to comprehend what is being said. Hearing reproof involves not only attending *to* what is being said but also intending *to obey* or *heed* what is being said. If this is the way you want your children to respond to reproof when they are grown, you must begin to teach them how to do

---

[1] Ibid., p. 393.

so now while they are young and while you have the rod to help drive out foolishness from their hearts (Prov. 22:15).

Is Spanking the Only Authorized Form of Discipline?

At this point you may be wondering whether or not the rod is the *only* biblically-authorized means of disciplining your child. Well, it is and it isn't. The rod *is* the only specific means the Bible designates when it addresses the discipline of children. Therefore, it should be used consistently with every child. However, as we have seen, the word *paideuo* (one of the most commonly used New Testament words for teaching children) is "training that has teeth in it." *Paideuo* is training that sees to it that the job gets done. It sometimes involves punishment or chastisement. In 1 Timothy 1:20 for example, Hymenaeus and Alexander were "delivered over to Satan so that they may be taught (*paideuo*) not to blaspheme." Christian parents may, therefore, within the confines of Scripture use other forms of discipline to augment the use of the rod. Moreover, older children who no longer are spanked may be chastised by other means as well. Spanking, then, (accompanied by doctrine, reproof, correction and disciplined-training in righteousness) is the primary means for disciplining children. Certain other forms of discipline that involve reward and punishment (also accompanied by doctrine, reproof, correction, and disciplined training in righteousness) may also be used in an ancillary fashion. But spanking, especially for younger children, probably should not be replaced often with other forms of punishment when children commit deliberate acts of disobedience.

> A rebuke goes deeper into one who has understanding
> Than a hundred blows into a fool.   (Prov. 17:10)

Unless and until this proverb is true of your child (until you are sure he is not a fool, but truly is a man of understanding), you will need to use both the rod[1] and reproof.

---

[1] The Rod: corporal punishment and/or ancillary forms of chastisement. Although I do not believe "the rod" is to be taken figuratively (the rod *is* cor-

Developing a Biblically-based Procedure for Spanking

There are dozens of books on the market today which purport to give biblical guidelines for the corporal discipline of children. In my years of studying the Scriptures, I've yet to find the exact biblical procedure for spanking. I don't believe one exists. Rather, I believe that God has provided some basic directives and guiding principles, a framework around which we as Christian parents may customize our approach to this process. Or, to use another analogy, I believe the Bible gives the exact same skeleton on which each set of Christian parents must add muscle and skin to create a unique embodiment of biblical discipline.

In providing the following material, I do not wish to impose on any reader's conscience that which is not clearly taught in the Scriptures. Too much of that kind of parenting "legalism" already abounds today. Rather, I offer basic guidelines in the form of questions to help you construct your own individual biblically-based approach to the use of the rod. Although the answers to some of these questions may overlap at points, thinking through each question will help ensure a more thorough and complete evaluation. I pray that they will be helpful as you develop your own biblically-based program which incorporates both the rod and the Scriptures.

1.　Is the concept of "teaching in the milieu" understood and practiced in your home?

Are your children aware that you and your spouse are committed to teaching them about God and His ways every teachable moment of every day? Do you conscientiously and faithfully apply Deuteronomy 6:6-9 in your parenting? Do your children understand that one of your most important parental responsibilities is to teach them God's Word and its application to every circumstance and contingency in their lives?

---

poral punishment), there may be times when other forms of discipline can rightly be combined with reproof, and thus the spirit of Proverbs 29:15 can be fulfilled.

2. Do you talk regularly about why you must spank your children when they disobey?

Do your children know that you are acting under the authority of God and that whether or not to spank is not your choice? This is an important concept. You spank your children because God tells you to. A decision to spank or not to spank should not be left to your moods or whims. If a spanking is necessary for correction, you are not biblically free to decide *not* to spank. You must work hard to let your children know this. If your child has defiantly broken God's law, you do not have the right to say that you are too busy, tired, etc., to do what God has called you to do.[1] It is the Lord's instruction, not yours (cf. Eph. 6:1-4). Likewise, spanking should not be used for selfish parental reasons such as to ventilate frustration, to vindicate an offense, to stimulate good behavior for your own convenience, or to save face in public when your child embarrasses you by his behavior.

3. Is verbal confrontation ongoing?

If you engage in more instances of physical discipline than verbal discipline, you are probably (almost certainly) not doing enough verbal instruction and confrontation.[2] Do you attempt to deal with sinful behavior whenever it is necessary to do so? Or do you, like so many, allow your child to commit the same transgression again and again without reproof until finally, in a fit of sinful anger, you overreact out of selfish motives and discipline him without patiently explaining to him the appropriate passages of Scripture? Although the context of Paul's exhortation to Timothy is not the parent-child relationship, his words in principle, are applicable to every Christian parent: "preach the Word; be ready [prepared] in season [and] out of season; reprove, rebuke, exhort, with great patience and instruction" (2 Tim. 4:2).

---

[1] As I've already mentioned, this is not to imply that spanking is the only biblical disciplinary option when your child sins.
[2] Beware of excessive reasoning (especially with young children) which may be counterproductive to the disciplinary process.

4. Is your communication "always with grace"?

Teaching in the milieu means teaching with pleasant words (cf. Prov. 16:20-24). Spanking falls in the context of teaching in the milieu (it's a part of the process of child discipline). Unrighteous anger that leads to personal attack or animosity between you and your child has no place in biblical discipline. "The anger of a man does not achieve the righteousness of God" (James 1:20). Pleasant words about spanking in a setting when spanking is not in view lets your child know that it is God's agenda you are pursuing. The matter is between the child and God. His parents are acting as God's agent. When the child sins, it is often appropriate to be stern and forceful in your tone. However, it is important to remember to use only *righteous* anger that is appropriate to bring the occasion for spanking to biblical conclusion. The purpose and goal of biblical discipline is the well-being of your children and the glory of God. In this context, even words of admonishment will later be discerned as pleasant because they are life-giving.[1]

5. Do you take your child to a private place where he can be dealt with in privacy?

If the child's transgression was committed publicly, it *may* be appropriate to rebuke him publicly.[2] However, spanking should be done privately, without unnecessary embarrassment. Be careful not to violate either the spirit or the letter of Matthew 18:15, "And if your

---

[1] In the current political debate between those who believe in corporal punishment and those who do not, so called "scientific studies" are often cited by those who are against it. One wonders how compelling such a study would be if all those subjects who were observed were trained in and truly employed biblical spanking methodologies. I have it on good authority that no such study has yet been done.

[2] Paul publicly rebuked Peter for being a hypocrite in the presence of those who had observed his hypocrisy (Gal. 2:11-14). Also, Christ's questioning of Peter in the presence of the other disciples about the degree of his love for Him was done the first time the two had an opportunity to speak to each other after Peter boasted of his loyalty to Christ before those same disciples (Matt. 26:33; John 21:15-18).

brother sins, go and reprove him in private; if he listens to you, you have won your brother."

6. **When you believe that physical discipline is necessary in addition to the ongoing verbal instruction, do you insure that your child understands exactly *what* he has done wrong and *that* you must spank him for his actions?**

Let me again emphasize the importance of your child understanding that you are not being capricious or cavalier with your spankings. You must not simply drag him off to a room and spank him without first spending time *communicating* to him about his sin. Let me say it again. If you are spending more time spanking your child than you are instructing him from the Bible, something is askew with your methodology of discipline. If you are depending more on the spanking procedure than you are on your loving relationship with your child to produce the desired change, you're not practicing biblical parenting (and you're almost certainly not spending enough time with him). Such attitudes are all too common in today's business-oriented society and betray all manner of unbiblical parental attitudes (such as misplaced priorities, selfishness, and impatience). Of course, your child should be told that you have no option but to spank him because God's Word requires it.

As a principle of effective teaching, it is often better to encourage your student to identify for himself what is to be learned, rather than to spoon feed him every morsel of truth. By motivating your child to pinpoint his own transgressions of God's law, you help cement into his mind the truth about the sin for which you are going to spank him. This can best be done by the use of questions: questions like "Honey, exactly what did you do that was wrong?" or "In what way(s) did you sin against God just now?" focus the child's attention where it should be focused—on his relationship with the Lord. Of course, if the child cannot identify his sin correctly, you will need to help him. But whether he comes up with the right answer by himself or you provide him with the answer, the exercise of self-discovery will likely enable him to better remember the lesson.

Bruce Ray, in his insightful book *Withhold Not Correction*, makes another very good point about having the child identify his sinful behavior with specific terminology.[1]

> Have him *be specific*. Don't settle for "I disobeyed," or "I did something I wasn't supposed to do." Those very general answers don't tell us that he really understands. They may simply be his reaction to the circumstances. He knows that he is disciplined when he disobeys. He is being disciplined; therefore he must have disobeyed. If he does not know *specifically* what he is being corrected for, he will not be corrected. If he doesn't understand, you can count on him to do it again.

7. Does your child understand in biblical terminology how he has sinned against God?

Did you relate your child's misbehavior to Scripture? Asking questions like "Johnny, do you know what the Bible says about what you did/said?" or "Do you remember the Scripture verse we all memorized as a family that addressed what you just did/said?" Give him an opportunity to interpret his own sin biblically. Does your child understand the connection between what he did (or didn't do) and the biblical command which he transgressed? That is the question you want to have answered (if at all possible) in the affirmative before proceeding with any form of discipline. Be patient and remind yourself often that your child is not being disciplined because he somehow made life miserable for you, but because he sinned against God.

Another benefit of using biblical terminology in the disciplinary process is that it makes finding the biblical solution (the correction and the disciplined training in righteousness) easier. As any true biblical counselor will tell you, "you cannot solve a problem biblically until you first identify that problem using biblical terminology." You'll never find the biblical solution for *rebellion*, *anger*, or *insubordination* by looking up (even) in the most exhaustive concordance the term *Oppositional Defiance Disorder*.[2]

---

[1] *Withhold Not Correction*, p. 88.
[2] *Oppositional defiance disorder* is an increasingly popular diagnosis made

8. Do you secure the child's acknowledgment that the spanking is an appropriate course of action (required by the Scriptures) before he is spanked?

Here is yet another place where milieu teaching is beneficial. If, in non-disciplinary situations, you are talking with your children about what God requires of you, and you have exposed them to passages of Scripture that speak to their behavior, then you have provided a basis for accountability to the Scriptures. If your teaching has been consistent, your child will have to agree that he is in violation of God's law and that God's Word says he must be disciplined. Initially, this procedure may take a while. However, it is vitally important. You are God's agent acting on His behalf. You must help your child see that you are not spanking because you have been personally inconvenienced, but because you love him and want to obey God yourself. Regularly reviewing with your child those passages of Scripture that emphasize your responsibility as a parent to spank him (such as 1 Sam. 3:13; Prov. 13:24, 19:18, 22:15, 23:13, 14; 29:15; Heb. 5:4-11) will help place the focus of the discipline where it belongs—on obedience to God and His Word.

Another benefit of securing your child's acknowledgment is that he has the opportunity to appeal your course of action.[1] It is important that your child know he will have a fair hearing from you. The process of securing your child's acknowledgment that any pending discipline is just also allows you an opportunity to rethink what caused you to pursue discipline in the first place; are you angry, out of control, did you make a snap judgment? Of course, the purpose for getting your child to acknowledge the necessity of a spanking is not to seek his approval. Rather, it is to make him aware that God's Word (including its judgments against sin and its instructions about the use of the rod) must be obeyed. If you have made an error in judgment, you will be

---

by many "so-called" mental health professionals as described in the DSM-IV (the Diagnostic and Statistical Manual of the American Psychiatric Association).

[1] See "Chapter 12: The Appeal Process" in *The Heart of Anger* for instructions on training children in the use of the appeal process.

able to correct it here. If you haven't, you have taught the child that you are acting on God's behalf.

9. Do you use a practiced and predictable method to spank the child?

Consistency is important. This consistency lets the child know that he is not a victim of whim or a bad day at the office. You are acting as God's agent, under His authority, with equity, consistency, and in an orderly fashion. As my friend Jay Younts puts it in his parenting course:

> The spanking must be sufficiently robust to make an impression. If you have followed [these] guidelines... and your child is still angry and sullen after the spanking, you probably have not spanked hard enough or long enough. Remember, retribution is not the goal here. It is not enough just to create a negative experience for the child. This should also be a positive, building experience for you and your child. Spankings that are too short may leave a child sullen, angry, and more resilient to future spankings. Another indicator of a spanking that is too short is if the child does not really seem changed or repentant even though he may have been wailing... when spanked. It is possible the child has learned what crying level will cause you to stop spanking. If this is the case, the wailing is not from pain but from an attempt to manipulate you.

In *The Heart of Anger*, I made an analogy between parents who discipline their children out of anger and Balaam.[1]

> "When the donkey saw the angel of the LORD, she lay down under Balaam; so Balaam was angry and struck the donkey with his stick. And the LORD opened the mouth of the donkey, and she said to Balaam, 'What have I done to you, that you have struck me these three times?' Then

---

[1] *The Heart of Anger*, p. 48.

Balaam said to the donkey, 'Because you have made a mockery of me! If there had been a sword in my hand, I would have killed you by now'" (Num. 22:27-29).

When Balaam became angry at his donkey for not meeting his expectations, he struck the beast with a stick. Balaam went on to say that if he had had a sword he would have killed the donkey. Children are not beasts. Angry parents may be guilty of treating them as such when their anger is out of control. Several parallels can be made between Balaam's sinful anger and a parent out of control. I shall only mention a few.

First, Balaam struck the donkey in haste before he had collected all of the relevant data. Before parents jump to hasty and unfounded conclusions and discipline children for the wrong reason, they must be certain they have all the facts.

Second, Balaam struck the donkey because the donkey embarrassed him. Parents should be certain that their motivation for discipline is biblical, not selfish. To discipline a child for selfish reasons, such as embarrassment or unfulfilled expectations, rather than for sin is vindictive and abusive.

Third, Balaam was out of control. (He would have killed his faithful donkey if he had had the means to do it!) Parents should discipline their children only when their anger is under control and they are not likely to harm them.

Purposing to use only practiced and predictable methods of spanking helps prevent these types of hasty and abusive acts of vengeance during the disciplinary process.

10. Do you proclaim the Gospel to the child?

Sometimes the milieu of a spanking becomes a tremendous opportunity to impress upon an unregenerate child his need for Christ's forgiveness, as well as his inability to consistently obey the Bible (and his parents) apart from the indwelling Holy Spirit. If he is a believer, this is often a good time to help him see his need to depend on God's Spirit in conjunction with God's Word to bring about lasting change.

11. Do you discuss with your child how he could have handled the problem differently by following God's directives in the Bible? (Do you use the Gumnazo Principle?)

Since repentance involves both a change of one's mind and a correction of one's ways (cf. Is. 55:6-7), instructing your child about various biblical alternatives to the behavior for which he is being spanked is an essential element of the discipline process.

- "How could you have communicated your displeasure with my decision without being so disrespectful?"
- "Can you think of a way you can 'overcome evil with good' rather than being vindictive if Sally embarrasses you that way again?"
- "What would have been a better way to respond to your teacher when she falsely accused you in front of the whole class?"
- "Can you think of a more truthful answer to that question?"
- "Let's try to come up with three biblical options from which you could choose the next time you find yourself in that kind of situation."

After you have discussed alternative behaviors, if possible, consider discussing alternative ways to think the next time he is faced with a similar set of circumstances.

- "How should a Christian think—according to the Bible—when he is afraid of telling the truth?"
- "What should you have said to yourself the moment you realized you were...."

Then, if you can assist him to identify any sinful desires (motives) that carried him away and enticed him into the sin (James 4:1), help him to discover what he could have desired according to Scripture that would have prevented the sinful behavior (and the spanking) from happening.

- "What were you wanting (longing for, craving, or seeking your happiness in) when you did what you did?"

- "What should you have wanted (longed for, craved, or sought your happiness in) when you did what you did?" [1]

12. Do you use the Scriptures to correct and instruct your child in righteousness?

Role playing the scenario with your child will often enable him to understand more clearly what the Bible requires of him. Providing him with the biblical alternative(s) to his sinful behavior is essential for true *gumnazo* training. If he is able, allow him to suggest the appropriate alternative(s).

"The Bible says, 'Let your speech always be with grace, seasoned, [as it were], with salt, so that you may know how you should respond to each person.' I don't think you quite 'know how you ought to answer' your sister when she does things that annoy you. Let's practice this again, but this time I want you to respond to her so that your speech has a little less salt and a lot more grace. Perhaps if you said it this way…"

13. Do you require the child to make any necessary restitution to other offended parties?

This involves asking for forgiveness from those against whom he has sinned. If the sin was a public sin, a public confession might even be in order. Restitution also may involve replacing items that were damaged or destroyed, repaying money that has been stolen, or confessing and correcting lies that were told.

14. Do you comfort and pray with your child when you are finished spanking the child? (Do you hold the child and tell him of your love for him?)

While holding your child, it is often good to remind him again why you spanked him (because God tells you to spank him and because He will "spank" you if you don't spank him). If you've not yet

---

[1] Let me again refer you to *The Heart of Anger* for additional assistance with this procedure.

done so, you can use this time to call your child to faith and repentance. These moments can be very special and precious.

A prayer could be said for the child to know God and for God to work in his heart. Such a prayer should specifically reference the reason for the spanking. This is an ideal time to teach children their need of a Savior—they cannot obey in their own strength. Depending on the age and maturity of the child, encourage him to pray also, asking for the same things, as well as forgiveness for his sin.

When you are finished, you and your child should be comforted, happy, refreshed, and secure with each other. Leaving a child in a weepy, angry, fearful, frustrated state after discipline is both cruel and counterproductive. In such cases the child has not learned to trust Christ but rather to fear you. Remember, God's discipline produces good fruit (Heb. 12:11). Your selfish discipline will produce alienation.

Sin is serious. Your children must know this. In Christ there is freedom from sin and resolution of conflict. The Bible provides the ways to peace for your children. Spankings can be traumatic and tear down, or they can be positive and build up. Loving communication throughout the disciplinary process is perhaps the best way to ensure that the rod is being used constructively and not destructively. My prayer for you as you have read this chapter is that you might be convicted of any need you may have to communicate the Scriptures to your children at every possible juncture. May God give you the wisdom, grace and patience to effectively and consistently minister the *rod* and *reproof* to your children in love.

Make use of the Word of God in prosperity, adversity, darkness, seasons of doubt, times of perplexity, and your entire walk. Nothing can befall you, nor is there any duty in which you must engage where the Word of God would not provide you with comfort, peace, counsel, and direction. "Thy testimonies also are my delight and my counselors; I have chosen the way of truth: Thy judgments have I laid before me; Thy word is a lamp unto my feet, and a light unto my path; Thy testimonies have I taken as an heritage for ever: for they are the rejoicing of my heart" (Ps. 119:24, 30, 105, 111, KJV).

Wilhelmus à Brakel, Th.F.[1]

---

[1] *The Christian's Reasonable Service*, Volumes I and II, (Simpsonville, SC: Christian Classics Foundation, 1997).

chapter seven

Learning to Use Life's Instruction Manual

"There is no way I can do what you've suggested doing in this book without knowing the Bible better than I do! I'm going to have to know what God says and where in the Bible He says it. In fact, I really wonder if I even know the Bible well enough to do what you're recommending. And I really don't have a clue how or where to find all this stuff in Scripture."

If you've been thinking thoughts like these at various places in your journey through the pages of this book, I certainly can sympathize with your sense of being overwhelmed. Ours is an awesome calling and responsibility. But the truth is, biblical parenting takes work. If you want to be an effective biblical parent, you'll have to invest time and effort in studying God's Word yourself. Timothy knew the Scriptures from childhood presumably because his grandmother and mother knew them before he did (2 Tim. 1:5). The faith that dwelt in Him first dwelt in them. It is again worth noting in Deuteronomy 6, that the command for parents to know the Scriptures themselves precedes the command to teach them diligently to their children.

> And you shall love the Lord your God with all your heart and with all your soul and with all your might. And these words, which I am commanding you today, shall be on your heart; and you shall teach them diligently to your sons and shall talk of them when you sit in your house and when you walk by the way and when you lie down and when you rise up. (Deut. 6:5-7)

God's words must first be in your heart before you can rightly expect them to dwell in the hearts of your children. To put it in the vernacular of the Apostle Paul, "the word of Christ" must first "richly dwell in you with all wisdom" before you will be able to "teach" and "admonish" others (Col. 3:16).

Sadly, many professing Christians don't even make time in their daily schedule to study the Scriptures for themselves, let alone teach it to their children. Yet Scripture is filled with references that should motivate us to spend time daily studying the Bible. Job said, "I have treasured the words of His mouth more than my necessary food" (Job 23:12). David records the blessedness of the man whose "delight is in the law of the Lord," and who meditates "in His law...day and night" (Ps. 1:2). The author of Psalm 119 declares,

> Oh, how I love Your law!
> It [is] my meditation all the day.
> You, through Your commandments, make me wiser than
>   my enemies;
> For they [are] ever with me.   (vv. 97, 98, NKJV)

Quoting Deuteronomy 8:3, Jesus said, "It is written, 'Man shall not live on bread alone, but on every word that proceeds out of the mouth of God'" (Matt. 4:4). Peter commands, "Like newborn babes, long for the pure milk of the word, that by it you may grow in respect to salvation" (1 Pet. 2:2). The Bereans "were more noble-minded than those in Thessalonica, for they received the word with great eagerness, examining the Scriptures daily, [to see] whether these things [the apostles' doctrine] were so" (Acts 17:11).

The saints in the passages you've just read took Bible study seriously. They saw it as (and made it) a priority. Geoffrey Thomas, in his excellent little booklet entitled *Reading the Bible*, put it well.[1]

> The Christian Life is paved with the best intentions of reading the Scriptures regularly, and also with many broken resolutions and disappointments. Jesus exhorts us to search the Scriptures [*John 5:39*]; that is, we are to ransack the Word of God, to pore over it, to subject it to every kind of analysis, to grasp its every shade of meaning. We are to be obsessed with a desire to understand it.

---

[1] Geoffrey Thomas, *Reading the Bible* (Edinburgh: Banner of Truth Trust, 1980), p. 6.

This passionate concern is never to become incidental or secondary. It should be a priority in the Christian life, an activity around which our existence revolves.

So, rather than trying to squeeze the Bible into your daily schedule, like so many, shouldn't you plan your schedule around God's Word? Do you set aside time every day to eat, shower, shave, or groom yourself in a variety of other ways? Do you not place on your daily agenda a variety of other "important" things that must be done each day? If you schedule time for all these "necessary" things, shouldn't you make time for life's ultimate priority: worshiping God through Bible study and prayer? Are you like Martha, who was "distracted with all her preparations" and who was "worried and bothered about so many things" (Luke 10:40-42), or are you like Mary, who knew that only a few things in life are necessary—really only one: to sit at Christ's feet and hear His Word? I trust if you do not already do so, you will begin *today* to make personal Bible study (and prayer) your top priority each and every day.

There is no spiritual shortcut, no instant "Scripture knowledge pill" you can take, no "wiffle dust" that can be sprinkled over you to give you a Bible college or seminary education in ten weeks. You must learn God's Word little by little, line by line, precept by precept. But the good news is: you can learn as you go. If you haven't started on your way, you must get going today.

"But," you say, "I don't know how or even where to begin to study the Bible." Before offering to help with your dilemma, let me first say that many volumes have been written to assist Christians in their study of God's Word by people much more knowledgeable on this subject than I am (and in much more exhaustive ways than can be done in this little book). The majority of these fine works are designed to help people with inductive Bible study (exegesis),[1] but relatively few exist that teach people how to use the Bible as an instruction manual for living. What I would like to give you here are a few practical suggestions and

---

[1] Exegesis (the science of elucidating the meaning of a Bible text) must be balanced by systematic theology (the systematizing of everything the Bible has to say on a given topic into a cohesive study) and vice versa.

tools[1] that will help you go to the Scriptures that address the problems
in your child's life. Complete information on each resource is provided
in Appendix F: "Selective Bibliography of Helpful Resources"
(p. 158).

A Crash Course in Biblical Problem Solving

What follows in this section is an approach to going from a particular problem in your life, or the life of your child, to the Bible for the
purpose of finding a proper diagnosis and solution. It is a crash course
in solving problems biblically, not an exhaustive treatise on the subject.[2] This technique for discovering the biblical solution(s) to a problem in life is certainly not the only, or necessarily the best, one. If you
have a system that works better, you should probably stick with it.

Before we proceed, however, I must warn you about something.
Please *do not attempt to implement this system unless you have at least
a basic knowledge of Bible interpretation.* A person can find anything
he wants to find in the Bible and make it say whatever he wants it to
say if he is not committed to proper principles of biblical hermeneutics. Hermeneutics is the science of Bible interpretation. As a science,
it recognizes laws governing how the meaning of a particular portion
of Scripture is realized. It is beyond the scope of this book to explain
these laws, but I have included in Appendix F: "Selective Bibliography
of Helpful Resources" (p. 158) a list of books on the subject that
should help you better understand the science of hermeneutics and
assist you in cultivating the necessary skills. For one of the simplest
and most concise treatments see chapters 8 through 10 of *What to Do
on Thursday.*[3]

To keep things as simple as possible, I'm going to give you a small
list of problem-solving questions that will help direct you to the appro-

---

[1] What follows is certainly *not an exhaustive list* of suggestions or Bible
study tools but rather some I've personally found very helpful in my own
attempts to discover and systematize life issues.

[2] Jay E. Adams, *What to Do on Thursday* (Woodruff, SC: TIMELESS TEXTS).
This is one of those rare books that explains in great detail how to go to the
Scripture to find solutions (answers) for specific problems (questions) in life.

[3] *Ibid.*

priate portions of Scripture necessary to do the job of 2 Timothy 3:16. As with the questions in the last chapter on the use of the rod, keep in mind that some of your answers may overlap.

Question #1. Have I identified the problem in biblical terms?
Allow me to say it one more time: a problem cannot be solved biblically until it is first diagnosed in biblical terminology. The operative phrase is found in 1 Corinthians 2:13, "not in words taught us by human wisdom but in words taught by the Spirit, *expressing spiritual truths in spiritual words*" (NIV, emphasis added). You'll probably not find the word *shy* in many popular English Bible translations. What you will find in the Bible, however, are the two most common root causes of shyness: *pride* and *fear*. Similarly, the term *strong-willed*[1] is not a biblical construct—*self-willed* is (Titus 1:7; 2 Pet. 2:10). Be careful also about so-called "medical diagnoses," such as Attention Deficit Disorder[2] which typically has as its two chief symptoms the expression of sinful *anger* and lack of *self-control*.

Force yourself to think biblically. Don't settle for less than God's interpretation of the problem. Even if you're convinced there is an organic (physiological) basis[3] for your (child's) behavior, try to identify the attending sin issues associated with that problem. The world

---

[1] To a certain extent I want my children to be *strong-willed*. That is, I desire for them to have such control over their own *will* that they obey God even when others (the world), their own feelings (the flesh), or Satan (the Devil) tempt them to do otherwise. Under no circumstances, however, do I want them to be *self-willed*.

[2] Attention Deficit Disorder is another (non-organic disease) construct from the DSM-IV (Diagnostic and Statistical Manual-fourth edition) of the American Psychiatric Association.

[3] There may be legitimate medical problems that have as their side effects greater temptation to sin. Like Job, who when he was afflicted in his body (see Job chapter 2) was more easily tempted to sin, so physical illness can make it easier for people to sin—and harder for them to obey God. Such sin however, cannot be excused—especially for professing Christians, for "where sin abounded, grace abounded much more" (Rom. 5:20, NKJV). God promises the Christian that He will provide him with the grace (the supernatural power and desire) to not sin—even when he is ill, or tired (cf. 1 Cor. 10:13). This grace is available for both believing children and their parents!

and even other Christians may have settled for less than a biblical interpretation, but you must keep searching for the right diagnosis if you want to find a lasting biblical solution.

Question #2. Have I gotten to the deepest level of the problem rather than simply identifying its symptoms?

It is important when dealing with sin, to not focus on the symptomatic problems when more serious underlying attitude issues of the heart and character flaws exist. Of course, even symptomatic sin problems (such as episodes of biting sarcasm or outbursts of temper) are grievous to God and must be corrected. But, if you stop there without looking for and addressing any deeper problems (such as a character deficiency, an idolatrous inordinate desire, or a sinful thought pattern), other surface problems are likely to develop—even if the original one doesn't reoccur.

Look for common denominators to all of your child's sin. What sinful attitude or characterological sin is associated with the majority of his transgressions? How much of his behavior is rooted in attitudinal sins such as selfishness, pride, slothfulness, or anger? Is he a "lover of pleasure" or "lover of money" or "lover of man's approval?" Does he savor the things of man rather than the things of God? Does he value the things that God values as much as he should? Does he value things that God doesn't value more than he should? Is his behavior characteristic of a particular kind of person in the Bible (such as an angry man, a fool, a sluggard, a liar, or an idolater)? Or is his behavior simply indicative of the fact that he is not truly a Christian? These are the kinds of questions a thoughtful parent asks himself and his child in the process of correcting him.

Question #3. Have I identified both that which must be "put off" and that which must be "put on?"

As we have seen, the biblical process of change is twofold. Sinful behavior must not only be put off, it must also be replaced with the appropriate biblical alternative(s). By the time you've answered questions one and two, chances are you've already identified the "put-off" part of the equation. What must be done next is to determine exactly what is to replace the sinful behavior.

I often use the following illustration with my counselees when explaining the put-off/put-on dynamic. Taking hold of a glass which sits next to a pitcher of cold water on my desk, I say, "This glass represents your heart." After filling the glass nearly full with water, I continue, "If I wanted to empty this glass in a way that would make it difficult for someone to come along and refill it, I'd have to do more than simply empty it. What I'd do is begin filling the glass with something heavier than the water—such as marbles or perhaps another dense fluid like Liquid Plumber. As I added the heavier substance to the water it would sink to the bottom of the glass. As the glass began to fill from the bottom," I ask, "What would happen to the water?"

"It would be displaced and begin to spill out over the top of the glass," comes the typical reply.

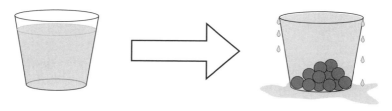

"Exactly! And, that's the way it is with the sin in our life. We displace the sin in our life (and heart) *by* replacing it with something better (or biblically heavier) than the sin."

In dependence on the Spirit, we replace rotten words with edifying words (Eph. 4:29), ungodly behavior with godly behavior, sinful thoughts with righteous thoughts, selfish motives with loving motives, bad attitudes with good ones, etc. But the first step is to figure out exactly what sin is to be removed and then what virtue must be substituted in its place. Remember, Christians don't break habits—pagans do. We replace sinful habits with righteous ones. Christian parent, if you're not building into your children the biblical alternative to the sin you're trying to correct, you're simply not training them biblically.

Question #4. Are there any directives in Scripture that must be obeyed, in order to solve the problem?
Sometimes the answer to a problem is clearly delineated in the Bible. That is, in order to solve the problem, specific scriptural commands

must be obeyed. Suppose for example, your child comes home from school with a report of a serious sin that one of his Christian friends has committed against him (one that can neither be *overlooked* according to Proverbs 19:11, nor *covered* by love as Peter suggests in 1 Peter 4:8). The solution to this kind of problem is specifically addressed in at least two New Testament passages.

> Be on your guard! If your brother sins, rebuke him; and if he repents, forgive him. And if he sins against you seven times a day, and returns to you seven times, saying, "I repent," forgive him.   (Luke 17:3, 4)

> And if your brother sins, go and reprove him in private; if he listens to you, you have won your brother. But if he does not listen [to you], take one or two more with you, so that BY THE MOUTH OF TWO OR THREE WITNESSES EVERY FACT MAY BE CONFIRMED.
>   (Matt. 18:15, 16)

In cases like this, the biblically-directed solution[1] will usually involve teaching your child about these passages (if he is not already familiar with them[2]) and helping him devise a plan to implement some kind of loving confrontation with (in the hope of granting forgiveness to) his offending brother. In most cases, it is better to instruct him in this way *before* you involve yourself directly in the conflict. The Bible is filled with directed counsel for very specific kinds of problems. Additionally, there is a plethora of scriptural commands which, if not followed, will not only displease God but also produce painful consequences. Sometimes the solution to life's problems is found by simply beginning to obey certain clear biblical directives.

Question #5. Are there any principles in Scripture from which a solution to the problem can be derived?

Sometimes the solution to a particular problem is not clearly delin-

---

[1] Jay E. Adams, in *What to Do on Thursday*, refers to these as biblically-directed solutions.

[2] Because each child has to deal with other little sinners on a regular basis, I believe these two passages should be taught and explained to every child as soon as possible.

eated in the Scriptures and must therefore be derived from appropriate biblical principles. These are sometimes referred to as *biblically-derived solutions*. A biblically derived solution is one that is devised by the Christian using Scriptural principles in order to achieve a biblical goal for which no explicit directives are given in the Bible.

Suppose after asking your child a serious question, you get a rather arrogant reply in response. One way to begin solving that problem would be to work Proverbs 15:28a into the solution. Perhaps you'd say it this way:

"Honey, that was not the way a 10-year-old boy ought to be answering his father—it was too insolent (cf. Psalm 75:5). The Bible says that *the heart of the righteous ponders how to answer.* Let's see how many more appropriate (humble) responses to my question we can come up with between the two of us in the next five minutes."

Or, what if your teenage son starts coming to you repeatedly, complaining that he never has enough money. Perhaps a biblically-derived solution such as this might help:

"Son, the book of Proverbs identifies over a dozen things that lead people into poverty. In fact, did you know that Jesus had more to say about money than He did about heaven and hell combined? Why don't you and I break out a concordance (or the computer Bible) and see if perhaps you're violating some of God's many principles of finance."

Suppose you're trying to help your child solve the common problem of not remembering (forgetting) to do those things which he is supposed to do. You could approach this using a number of biblically-directed solutions.

- You could encourage him to improve his attentiveness by explaining the principle found in Hebrews 2:1, the closer we pay attention the less likely we are to forget—"For this reason we must pay much closer attention to what we have heard, lest we drift away [from it]."

- You might help him make and memorize a list of those things he has most consistently forgotten to do, much like Peter did in the first chapter of his second epistle.

> Now for this very reason also, applying all diligence, in your faith supply moral excellence, and in [your] moral excellence, knowledge; and in [your] knowledge, self-

control, and in [your] self-control, perseverance, and in [your] perseverance, godliness; and in [your] godliness, brotherly kindness, and in [your] brotherly kindness, love. For if these [qualities] are yours and are increasing, they render you neither useless nor unfruitful in the true knowledge of our Lord Jesus Christ. For he who lacks these [qualities] is blind [or] short-sighted, having forgotten [his] purification from his former sins.   (2 Pet 1:5-9)

- You can also regularly remind your child what his responsibilities are (review his list with him) in the milieu of life, not just at the moment he forgets, but just like Peter did with his list.

  Therefore, I shall always be ready to remind you of these things, even though you [already] know [them], and have been established in the truth which is present with [you]. And I consider it right, as long as I am in this [earthly] dwelling, to stir you up by way of reminder, knowing that the laying aside of my [earthly] dwelling is imminent, as also our Lord Jesus Christ has made clear to me. And I will also be diligent that at any time after my departure you may be able to call these things to mind.
  (2 Pet. 1:12-15)

- You might explain to him (in light of such verses as Deut. 8:11-20; Prov. 3:1 and Matt. 16:8-10) that although we all sometimes forget to fulfill our responsibilities, at some point (especially after being told repeatedly) we have a responsibility to remember and therefore 'failure to remember' is sin. (*You* shouldn't *forget* to explain to him what the consequences will be for future incidents of such forgetfulness.)
- You should consider allowing your child to suffer the natural consequences of his forgetfulness, reminding him that this too is according to biblical principle (cf. Prov.1:31 and Hebrews 12:5-11).
- You could also help him prepare a daily schedule (or check list) of all his responsibilities, and hold him accountable for fulfilling each task in accordance with Ephesians 5:15, 16, "Therefore be

careful how you walk, not as unwise men, but as wise, making the most of your time, because the days are evil."

Often both biblically-directed solutions *and* biblically-derived solutions are necessary in order to solve problems effectively. Let me give you one final word of caution: A *biblically-derived* solution must never be elevated to the place of a *biblically-directed* solution. To not distinguish between the two by raising a biblical *principle* to the level of a *command* is to run the risk of being legalistic. As I sometimes tell my counselees, "You need to read your Bible more regularly than you have been doing. Unless you have a better idea,[1] I *suggest* you begin with... Proverbs."

Question #6. Has anyone in Scripture ever faced the same (or a similar) situation?

Who in the Bible...

- Had rebellious children?
- Lost some possession that was dear to him?
- Handled guilt biblically? (unbiblically?)
- Was falsely accused?
- Was envious of the wicked?
- Was taken away from his parents?
- Couldn't get along with another Christian?
- Stole something and had to make restitution?
- Lied?
- Had brothers who mistreated him?
- Was depressed?
- Was anxious?
- Fell out of love with someone?

Some answers to these questions are found in the box on page 125.

---

[1] Of course, as a parent, some of your "suggested" solutions will be commands which your children must obey. If they believe they have a better idea, they may make a respectful appeal for your consideration.

The Bible not only contains commands and principles that are helpful for solving problems, it also contains a wealth of examples (good and bad) that give insight into the right and wrong ways of solving problems. It was for our assistance in solving life's dilemmas that these examples have been included in Holy Writ.

> For whatever was written in earlier times was written for our instruction, that through perseverance and the *encouragement* of the Scriptures we might have hope.
>
> (Rom. 15:4).

When you and your child are facing a problem, searching the Scriptures to see who else faced such a trial can be quite profitable (useful). As you study the examples of other men and women recorded in the Bible, ask yourself the following questions:

- What was done (if anything) to cause the problem?
- What was done to properly solve the problem?
- What was done to improperly solve the problem?

Question #7. Are there any promises in Scripture that can be claimed in relation to the problem?

Not only do you and your children need help in solving problems, you also need hope! That is where Scriptural promises come in. Some find it helpful to classify these into two categories: conditional promises and unconditional promises. Since there are fewer unconditional promises in the Bible than conditional ones, let's begin with those. By unconditional promises, I mean those promises in God's Word to which no strings are attached for the believer. They are ours to possess by virtue of our standing in Christ. Many of these have to do with the blessed eternal state (heaven) which has been prepared for those who have trusted in the substitutionary death of Christ on the cross. "And this is the promise which He Himself made to us: eternal life" (1 John 2:25; see also 1 John 3:2, Rev. 21:4).

There is another category of such unconditional promises worth mentioning in this context that has to do with God's commitment to perfect the character of his saints. "For I am confident of this very thing, that He who began a good work in you will perfect it until the day of Christ Jesus" (Phil. 1:6; see also Psalm 138:8; 1 Thess. 5:23,

---

Who in the Bible ...

(some answers for the questions of page 123)

- Had rebellious children?
  Eli, Job, Samuel, The father of the prodigal sons
- Lost some possession that was dear to him?
  Job, youngest prodigal son
- Dealt with guilt biblically? *David* (unbiblically? *Judas*)
- Was falsely accused? *Paul, Jesus, Joseph, Mordecai, Mary*
- Was envious of the wicked? *Asaph (Ps. 73)*
- Was taken away from his parents? *Moses, Daniel, Joseph*
- Couldn't get along with another Christian?
  Euodias & Syntyche, Paul & Mark
- Stole something and had to make restitution?
  Zaccheus, Onesimus
- Lied? *I still haven't located them all!*
- Had brothers who mistreated him? *Joseph, Abel, Esau, Jesus*
- Was depressed? *Elijah, Job, David*
- Was anxious (worried)? *Martha, wicked & slothful servant (in the parable of talents, Matt. 25)*
- Fell out of love with someone? *The Ephesian Church (in Rev. 2)*

---

24).[1] You can be sure, Christian parent, that God is much more committed to the sanctification process of your children than you are.

The second category of promises found in the Bible is conditional promises. A conditional promise is one that is predicated on the believer fulfilling some specific stipulation or prerequisite in order for the promise to be fulfilled by God. There are conditions you must first fulfill in order to receive whatever benefit has been pledged. These promises are especially useful in motivating us (and our children) to obey God. Look for some form of an "if/then" relationship—stated or implied: if (your responsibility), then (God will do so and so). The classic example of such a promise for children is Ephesians 6:1-3.

---

[1] Arguably another category of unconditional "promises" would be those verses in the Bible which speak of God's perfections (His attributes which, like Him, are unchangeable and can be relied on by faith).

> Children, obey your parents in the Lord, for this is right.
> Honor your father and mother (which is the first com-
> mandment with a *promise*), that it may be well with you,
> and that you may live long on the earth.

Other examples include Matthew 6:33, "seek first His kingdom
and His righteousness; and all these things shall be added to you," and
Galatians 5:16, "walk by the Spirit, and you will not carry out the
desire of the flesh." And while you're looking for promises, don't forget the negative ones (the warnings about sin's consequences) such as
Galatians 6:7, "Do not be deceived, God is not mocked; for whatever a
man sows, this he will also reap." Promises such as these can have
application to all four phases of 2 Timothy 3:16, and so can help you
motivate your children to strengthen their character.

Helpful Bible Study Tools

Another essential ingredient for using the Scriptures as an instruction manual for living (and parenting) is familiarity with a variety of
helpful Bible study tools.

Concordances—The first course of action for the English Bible
student is usually a Concordance. Concordances help you find the
location of specific words used in particular translations of the Bible.

TSK—Next to the concordance, the *Treasury of Scripture Knowledge* is the most valued resource in my library when it comes to locating Bible passages on various topics. Unlike a concordance, the *TSK*
(which is essentially a list of over a million cross-references) will help
you find verses that have to do with topics where the topic itself is not
mentioned by name in the verses. For example, suppose you wanted to
find out what the Bible has to say about lying. You could look up the
various cognates of the words, lie and deceive, but you would come far
short of locating many of the verses where various lies were told in
Scripture. To date, I've been able to identify over twenty *kinds* of lies
told by different individuals throughout Scripture. Think of that. There
are over twenty ways people have lied in the pages of Scripture, and
for many of these categories several biblical characters can be cited.[1]

---

[1] You might also be interested to know, Christian parent, that most of the lies

The TSK will be a valuable tool to help you run down those portions of Scripture that illustrate many topics you'll be studying in the process of training your children.

Topical Bibles—A volume such as *Naves Topical Bible* can provide a good many verses on a variety of child-related topics. There are also several topical arrangements of the book of Proverbs which can be quite useful for parenting.

Bible Dictionaries and Encyclopedias—Works such as the *International Standard Bible Encyclopedia* (ISBE) and the *Zondervan Pictorial Bible Dictionary* are useful in understanding the history and context of particular passages. Also, original language dictionaries such as *The Theological Wordbook of the Old Testament* and *The Theological Wordbook of the New Testament* are very helpful for understanding the broad and narrow meanings of particular words.

Bible Commentaries—Individual commentaries on specific books of the Bible are valuable not only to help you understand the meaning of particular passages, but also to check your own interpretation of them. If you don't already have one, I recommend that you purchase a commentary or two on the book of Proverbs, since, as a parent, you'll be relying on this book very heavily—especially during the teenage years. You may also want to obtain commentary sets that cover every book of the Bible (or most of them). Two of my favorites are John Calvin's *Commentary* and *The Expositors Bible Commentary* (both are also available on CD ROM). Many people also like *Matthew Henry's Commentary.*

Computer Bibles—The growing number of Bible software programs is at once staggering and exciting. If you have a computer, these resources will not only save you time and money, but they will also provide you with additional tools to help you interpret the Scriptures more accurately. The most reputable computer Bibles typically include concordances, topical Bibles, TSK, and at least one whole Bible commentary. Some also contain ISBE.

---

mentioned in the Bible successfully duped their victims—at least temporarily. A lie is a very hard thing to defend against biblically. For more information about this subject get my cassette tape *Dealing with Deception in Counseling.* available from Sound Word Associates.

Carefully Selected Puritan Authors—Among my favorite resources for understanding issues of sin, "not in words taught by human wisdom, but in those taught by the Spirit," are some of the Puritan writers. These men lived and ministered to people before the advent of modern clinical psychology and consequently wrote not about psychological disorders of the mind but about spiritual disorders of the soul. With rare exception,[1] there is no hint of today's psychobabble in their writings. I've found Puritan authors like Richard Baxter, William Gouge, Jeremiah Burroughs, Edward Reynolds, and Octavious Winslow both helpful and thought-provoking, especially when it comes to diagnosing problems biblically. Not only can writings from the Reformation/Puritan period be helpful, so can sermons from that time (if you can find them).

Other Helpful 2 Timothy 3:16 Tools—While you are strengthening your own ability to study the Bible, you may benefit from the work of others who have taken the time to locate and systematize portions of Scripture into helpful categories. The following resources are some that I have found especially helpful in my counseling ministry. (See Appendix F, p. 158, for information about the publishers.)

* *For Instruction in Righteousness* by Pam Forster
  "A topical guide for parents, listing Scripture on over 50 common areas of sin. Each chapter gives Bible verses that tell about the sin, what the Bible says will happen to a person who indulges in that sin, parallel ideas for discipline, simple, instructive object lessons based on Scriptural teaching about the sin, verses that explain how God blesses those who resist the sin, parallel ideas for rewards and encouragement, fully quoted memory verses, Bible stories that illustrate obedience and disobedience." Available in a spiral binding or in a loose-leaf notebook.
* *Homework Manual for Biblical Living* (Volumes 1 and 2) by Wayne Mack

---

[1] The most notable exception is their reliance on and belief in Hippocrates' theory of personality which you may know as "the four temperaments." There are other problems with some of the Puritans as well, so be very careful not to imbibe doctrinal deficiencies as you read.

These two books contain a variety of Bible studies and practical assignments for use with parents and older children.

- *Quick Scripture Reference for Counseling* by John G. Kruis
  This spiral-bound 8 × 6 inch book contains a variety of Scripture passages for 93 common problems/issues of life.
- *The Christian Counselor's New Testament* by Jay Adams
  A modern English version which brings out counseling nuances of the original languages. It also traces a list of common counseling topics throughout the New Testament.
- *What to Do on Thursday* by Jay Adams
  This book will provide you with a systematic approach for finding biblical solutions to life's problems.

Eureka!

As we come to the close of this little book, I'd like you to consider one final passage of Scripture. It's the first five verses of Proverbs Chapter two. As you read this section, please take note of the fourth verse. When you're finished, I'm going to ask you a few final questions.

1 My son, if you will receive my sayings,
   And treasure my commandments within you,
2 Make your ear attentive to wisdom,
   Incline your heart to understanding;
3 For if you cry for discernment,
   Lift your voice for understanding;
4 If you seek her as *silver*,
   And *search* for her as for hidden treasures;
5 Then you will discern the fear of the Lord,
   And discover the knowledge of God.

This passage addresses what must be done to acquire wisdom. It is the fear of the Lord (v. 5) that is the beginning of wisdom. My question is, "Why silver and not gold?" Why does it say to seek wisdom as *silver* rather than gold? Hasn't gold always been more precious and valuable than silver? The best answer to this question I've ever heard has to do with geological excavation. Whereas gold may occasionally be found on top of the earth, silver must always be mined—you have to *dig* for it (and you usually have to dig *deep* if you want to get silver). Christian parent, if you want to have those wise children spoken of in the first chapter of this book, you'll have to work hard to do what has been suggested in this final chapter. You'll have to dig, dig, dig into God's Word to mine out the treasures that will transform your children!

There is much more that could and should be written about the practical applications of 2 Timothy 3:16 to parenting. For the present, these few chapters will have to suffice. But now that you have some new ideas and hopefully a few more tools to do your own research, you'll soon be able to develop fresh and exciting applications of Scripture in all four of the "profitable" categories as you prayerfully depend on the Holy Spirit's illuminating ministry. May God bless you richly as you invest your time and effort to use the Bible more thoroughly and effectively in the Christian upbringing of your children.

Happy Hunting!

Happy Excavating!

appendix a
Scripture Texts
for Child Training

At some point in the process of reading this book, you have probably wondered how you were going to find the appropriate Scriptures necessary to do what you've learned. There really is no easy answer—no shortcut. In order to effectively do the job God called you to do, you must invest time and effort to know the Scriptures yourself. You must know *what the Bible says and where it says it.*

This appendix is intended to get you started in your study. It is not exhaustive either in the scope of potential childhood problems or in the extent of potential child-related passages of Scripture (cf. Psalm 119:96). All of the passages cited under each category may not hit the bull's eye for the need of your particular child, but they should at least hit the target. Your job will be to learn how to use the Scriptures with pinpoint precision, putting the cross hairs of the Word of God precisely in the center of the target. Like a brain surgeon, you must learn how to handle the scalpel of Scripture so as to cut out the cancer that has infected your patient before it metastasizes.

Child's Behavior/ Condition	Scripture Passages	Additional References
Anger	Let everyone be quick to hear, slow to speak [and] slow to anger; for the anger of man does not achieve the righteousness of God. James 1:19, 20	Prov. 14:29; 29:11 Eph. 4:26, 31-32 1 Cor. 13:4-5

Child's Behavior/ Condition	Scripture Passages	Additional References
Argumentation (back talking to parents)	A wise son [accepts his] father's discipline, But a scoffer does not listen to rebuke. Poverty and shame [will come] to him who neglects discipline, But he who regards reproof will be honored. Prov. 13:1, 18	Prov. 10:8, 15:1 James 1:19-20 Judg. 3
Bad Company (wrong friendships)	Do not be deceived: Bad company corrupts good morals. 1 Cor. 15:33	Prov. 1:10-19; 2:10-19; 9:6; 12:26; 13:20; 28:7 Heb. 12:15
Bitterness (resentment)	Pursue peace with all men, and the sanctification without which no one will see the Lord. See to it that no one comes short of the grace of God; that no root of bitterness springing up causes trouble, and by it many be defiled. Heb. 12:14-15	Prov. 26:24-26 Gal. 5:15 Eph. 4:31 1 John 2:9-11
Blameshifting	He who conceals his transgressions will not prosper, But he who confesses and forsakes [them] will find compassion. Prov. 28:13	Gen. 3:12-13 Exod. 32:21-24 Prov. 19:3 Matt. 7:1-5 James 1:13-15

Child's Behavior/ Condition	Scripture Passages	Additional References
Complaining	Do all things without complaining and disputing. Phil. 2:14 (NKJV)	Ps.19:14 1 Cor. 10:10 Eph. 4:29 Phil. 4:11-13
Covetousness (greed)	And He said to them, "Take heed and beware of covetousness, for one's life does not consist in the abundance of the things he possesses." Luke 12:15 (NKJV)	Prov. 15:16-17 Prov. 17:1 Col. 3:5 1 Tim. 6:6
Defiance	The eye that mocks a father, And scorns a mother, The ravens of the valley will pick it out, And the young eagles will eat it. Prov. 30:17	Deut. 21:18-21 1 Sam. 15:23 Prov. 15:32 Prov. 19:26 Prov. 29:1
Disobedience	Children, be obedient to your parents in all things, for this is well pleasing to the Lord. Col. 3:20	Ex. 20:12 Prov. 13:13 Prov. 30:17 Eph. 6:1, 2
Disorderliness	Let all things be done decently and in order. 1 Cor. 14:40 (NKJV)	1 Cor. 11:34 1 Cor. 15:23
Disrespect	Honor your father and mother (which is the first commandment with a promise), that it may be well with you, and thatyoumaylivelongontheearth. Eph. 6:2-3	Ex. 20:12; 21:15 Deut. 27:16 Prov. 3:35; 20:20; 30:17

Child's Behavior/ Condition	Scripture Passages	Additional References
Fear	When I am afraid, I will put my trust in Thee. Ps. 6:3	Ps. 18:6-7 Matt. 10:29-30 2 Tim. 1:7 1 Pet. 3:6, 13-14 1 John 4:18
Foolishness	Foolishness is bound up in the heart of a child; The rod of discipline will remove it far from him. Prov. 22:15	Ps. 107:17 Prov. 1:7; 10:1; 12:15, 16; 14:3, 16; 15:5, 20; 17:10, 12; 18:2, 6, 7; 19:29; 20:3; 22:15; 26:3 26:11, 12; 29:11
Forgetfulness	We must pay more careful attention, therefore, to what we have heard, so that we do not drift away. Heb. 2:1 (NIV)	Deut. 4:9 Prov. 4:20-23 2 Pet. 1:12-15 2 Pet. 3:1
Friendlessness	A man of [many] friends [comes] to ruin, But there is a friend who sticks closer than a brother. Prov. 18:24	Prov. 12:26; 17:17 John 15:13-15 1 Cor. 15:33 James 2:23, 4:4

Child's Behavior/ Condition	Scripture Passages	Additional References
Gossip	Not returning evil for evil, or insult for insult, but giving a blessing instead; for you were called for the very purpose that you might inherit a blessing. For, "Let him who means to love life and see good days Refrain his tongue from evil andhislipsfromspeakingguile." 1 Pet. 3:9-10	Prov. 11:13, 20:19, 26:20-22 Titus 3:1, 2 James 3:8-10, 4:11
Grief	"But because I have said these things to you, sorrow has filled your heart." John 16:6 (NKJV)	Lam. 3:31-33 John 11:25 Rom. 12:15 2 Cor. 7:10-11 Eph. 4:30
Guilt	He who conceals his transgressions will not prosper, But he who confesses and forsakes them will find compassion. Prov. 28:13	Acts 24:16 1 Cor. 4:14 Heb. 10:22 1 Pet. 3:16 1 John 1:9
Hypocrisy	If we say that we have fellowship with Him and [yet] walk in the darkness, we lie and do not practice the truth. I John 1:6	Matt 6:1-18, 7:3-5 1 Tim. 4:2 1 Pet. 2:1 James 3:17, 4:8
Idolatry	Little children, keep yourselves from idols. 1 John 5:21 (KJV)	Ex. 20:3 1 Cor. 10:7, 14

Child's Behavior/ Condition	Scripture Passages	Additional References
Impatience	Love is patient, love…bears all things, believes all things, hope all things, endures all things. 1 Cor. 13:4, 7	Heb. 6:15, 10:36 James 1:2-4 1 Pet. 1:13, 2:19-23
Impulsiveness (hastiness)	But the fruit of the Spirit is love, joy, peace, patience, kindness, goodness, faithfulness, gentleness, self-control; against such things there is no law. Gal. 5:22-23	Prov. 25:28, 29:11 Titus 2:10-11 1 Pet. 1:13 2 Pet. 1:5-6
Inappropriate Speech	Do not let any unwholesome talk come out of your mouths, but only what is helpful for building others up according to their needs, that it may benefit those who listen. Eph. 4:29 (NIV)	Prov. 10:31-32 Matt. 12:34-37 Col. 3:17; 4:6 1Thess. 5:11 James 3:2-8
Inattentiveness	Hear, [O] sons, the instruction of a father, And give attention that you may gain understanding. Prov. 4:1	Prov. 18:2, 13 Heb. 2:1 James 1:19
Insensitivity (to the needs and desires of others: lack of compassion)	But whoever has the world's goods, and beholds his brother in need and closes his heart against him, how does the love of God abide in him? I John 3:17	Is. 58: 7-10 Matt. 9:36, 14:14, 15:32, 20:34 1 Pet. 3:8

Child's Behavior/ Condition	Scripture Passages	Additional References
Intemperance (lack of self-control)	[Like] a city that is broken into [and] without walls is a man who has no control over his spirit. Prov. 25:28	Prov. 29:11, 16:32 1 Cor. 9:25-27 2 Pet. 1:5-6
Interrupting	A fool does not delight in understanding, But only in revealing his own mind. He who gives an answer before he hears, It is folly and shame to him. Prov. 18:2, 13	Eccl. 3:7 1 Cor. 13:5 Titus 2:6 1 Pet. 1:13
Judging Wrongfully (motives, disputable issues, the Law)	"Do not judge according to appearance, but judge with righteous judgment." John 7:24	Is. 11:3, 4 Matt. 7:1, 2 Rom.14:3, 4, 10-13 1 Cor. 4:3-5 James 4:11, 12
Jealousy/Envy	Love…is not jealous. 1 Cor 13:4	Prov. 14:30; 23:17; 27:4 Rom. 13:13 Gal. 5:26 1 Pet. 2:1, 2
Loneliness	[It is] good for a man that he should bear The yoke in his youth. Let him sit alone and be silent Since He has laid [it] on him. Lam. 3:27, 28	Ps. 37:4, 38:11 Lam. 3:24-40 John 16:32

Child's Behavior/ Condition	Scripture Passages	Additional References
Love of Approval (menpleasing)	Nevertheless many even of the rulers believed in Him, but because of the Pharisees they were not confessing [Him], lest they should be put out of the synagogue; for they loved the approval of men rather than the approval of God. John 12:42-43	Prov. 29:25 Matt. 23:5-7 Gal. 1:10 Col. 3:22
Love of Money	For the love of money is a root of all [kinds] [of] evil, for which some have strayed from the faith in their greediness, and pierced themselves through with many sorrows. 1 Tim. 6:10 (NKJV)	Matt. 6:24 2 Tim. 3:1-5
Love of Pleasure	What is the source of quarrels and conflicts among you? Is not the source your pleasures that wage war in your members? James 4:1	Prov. 21:17 2 Tim. 3:4
Love of Self	And He was saying to [them] all, "If anyone wishes to come after Me, let him deny himself, and take up his cross daily and follow Me. For whoever wishes to save his life will lose it, but whoever loses his life for My sake, he is the one who will save it. Luke 9:23-24	Matt. 20:26-28 1 Cor. 10:24 1 Cor. 13:5

Child's Behavior/ Condition	Scripture Passages	Additional References
Lying	Lying lips [are] an abomination to the Lord, But those who deal truthfully [are] His delight. Prov. 12:22 (NKJV)	Job 27:4 Prov. 6:16-19 Eph. 4:25 1 Pet. 3:10
Masturbation	But I say, walk by the Spirit, and you will not carry out the desire of the flesh. For the flesh sets its desire against the Spirit, and the Spirit against the flesh; for these are in opposition to one another, so that you may not do the things that you please. But if you are led by the Spirit, you are not under the Law. Gal. 5:16-18	Prov. 5:18-20 Matt. 5:27-28 Col. 3:5-6 2 Tim. 2:22 1 Thess. 4:3-4
Misuse of the Body (over/ undereating, uncleanness, etc.)	But I say, walk by the Spirit, and you will not carry out the desire of the flesh. For the flesh sets its desire against the Spirit, and the Spirit against the flesh; for these are in opposition to one another, so that you may not do the things that you please. But if you are led by the Spirit, you are not under the Law. Gal. 5:16-18	Rom. 8:5-8 Rom. 13:14 2 Cor. 7:1 1 Pet. 2:11

Child's Behavior/ Condition	Scripture Passages	Additional References
Pride	Young men, in the same way be submissive to those who are older. All of you, clothe yourselves with humility toward one another, because, "God opposes the proud but gives grace to the humble." Humble yourselves, there-fore, under God's mighty hand, that he may lift you up in due time. 1 Pet. 5:5-6	Prov. 8:13 Gal. 6:3-4 James 4:6 2 Tim. 2:24-26
Quarreling	What is the source of quarrels and conflicts among you? Is not the source your pleasures that wage war in your mem-bers? James 4:1	Prov. 13:10 1 Cor. 1:11-13 Phil. 2:1-11 1 Tim. 3:3
Rejection	Do not be overcome by evil, but overcome evil with good. Rom. 12:21	Ps. 35; Is. 53 Rom. 12:17-21 Eph. 4:31, 32
Slothfulness	Whether, then, you eat or drink or whatever you do, do all to the glory of God. 1 Cor. 10:31	Prov. 6:6-11 14:23; 19:15 20:13 26:13-16 2 Thess. 3:10
Stealing	Let him who stole steal no longer, but rather let him labor, working with [his] hands what is good, that he may have something to give him who has need. Eph. 4:28 (NKJV)	Ex. 20:15 Mt. 15:17-20 I Pet. 4:15

Child's Behavior/ Condition	Scripture Passages	Additional References
Selfishness	[Let] nothing [be] [done] through selfish ambition or conceit, but in lowliness of mind let each esteem others better than himself. Let each of you look out not only for his own interests, but also for the interests of others. Phil. 2:3-4 (NKJV)	Prov. 11:24-25 Rom. 12:20-21 Rom. 15:1 Gal. 5:13-15, 6:9 1 Pet. 4:9-11
Stinginess (not sharing)	And do not forget to do good and to share with others, for with such sacrifices God is pleased. Heb. 13:16 (NIV)	Prov. 11:24-25, 22:9 Luke 10:25-37 Eph. 4:28 I Tim. 6:18
Stubbornness (Insubordina- tion)	Children, obey your parents in the Lord for this is right. Eph. 6:1	1 Sam. 15:23 James 4:6
Teasing/ Jesting	Like a madman who throws Firebrands, arrows and death, So is the man who deceives his neighbor, And says, "Was I not joking?" Prov. 26:18-19	Prov. 12:18 Eph. 4:29; 5:4
Ungratefulness	In everything give thanks; for this is God's will for you in Christ Jesus. 1 Thess. 5:18	2 Tim. 3:2 Col. 3:15, 17, 4:2 Heb. 13:5

Child's Behavior/ Condition	Scripture Passages	Additional References
Unfaithfulness (not being dependable, reliable, or trustworthy)	Simply let your "Yes" be "Yes," and your "No," "No"; anything beyond this comes from the evil one. Matt. 5:37 (NIV)	Ps. 15:4-5 Prov. 6:1-5 Matt. 21:28-32 Col. 3:9
Unkindness	Let your speech always be with grace, as though seasoned with salt, so that you will know how you should respond to each person. Col. 4:6	Prov. 19:22 Luke 6:35 1 Cor. 13:4 Eph. 4:23, 29 Col. 3:12
Vindictiveness	See that no one repays another with evil for evil, but always seek after that which is good for one another and for all men. 1 Thess. 5:15	Prov. 20:22 Rom. 12:14-21 Eph. 4:26 Heb. 12:15
Withdrawing (clamming up)	[There is] a time to be silent, and a time to speak. Eccl. 3:7	1 Sam. 19:4-5, 25:24-42 Est. 4:13, 14, 7:4 Job. 32:4-22 Prov. 24:11, 12 31:8, 9 Acts 4:19, 20

Child's Behavior/ Condition	Scripture Passages	Additional References
Worry	Be anxious for nothing, but in everything by prayer and supplication, with thanksgiving, let your requests be made known to God; and the peace of God, which surpasses all understanding, will guard your hearts and minds through Christ Jesus. Finally, brethren, whatever things are true, whatever things [are] noble, whatever things [are] just, whatever things [are] pure, whatever things [are] lovely, whatever things [are] of good report, if [there] [is] any virtue and if [there] [is] anything praiseworthy—meditate on these things. Phil. 4:6-8 (NKJV)	Ps. 37:5 Matt. 6:25, 34 1 Pet. 5:6-7

appendix b
Questions That Help Bring Conviction

1. Do you know what God calls what you just did/said?
2. Do you realize that what you did is a sin? The Bible calls it
   _____.
3. Can you think of a more gracious (or other appropriate biblical term) way to say (or respond to) that?
4. What exactly did you do? (instead of "Did you do that?")
5. What went through your mind when you did/said that?
6. What did you want (long for, crave) when you did/said that?
7. Are you more concerned about pleasing yourself or pleasing God?
8. How exactly was God glorified by what you said/did?
9. Did you pray about that decision before you made it?
10. What was the biblical basis for that decision?
11. How did those words build up or minister grace to that person?
12. If I were to ask your teacher (or mother or sister or whoever observed the behavior in question) if what you did was right, what would she (or he) say?

Projects in Proverbs[1]

The book of Proverbs is especially suited for the milieu. It contains truisms that give guidance in a variety of areas—especially when dealing with people (one of life's greatest difficulties). Like a CD-ROM Bible program which may have printed on its surface only a few sentences but when inserted into a computer unfolds into many thousands (if not millions) of words, so each Proverb has much truth compacted and compressed into it. Someone has also likened this book to a piece of Jolly Rancher™ candy, which (unlike a piece of M&M™ candy) doesn't "melt in your mouth" but rather can be savored much longer as more and more flavor is extracted from it. This project, because of its emphasis on the application of truth to a vast array of contingencies, when done consistently, should give you and your children, over the course of time, an appreciation for the sufficiency of Scripture in every area of life: "To all perfection I see a limit; but Your commands are boundless" (Ps. 119:96, NIV).

This approach to studying the book of Proverbs can be used as an extended family time study or as a personal Bible study for parents and older children. It will probably take between 30 and 45 minutes once you get the knack of doing it.

1. **Come to the book of Proverbs with a question.**
"Is there something in your life (some problem, concern, or question) for which you want to find an answer in the Bible?" This step not only creates interest but it also underscores the fact that God's Word is meant to be used as a manual for living ("truth to be lived"— not merely "facts to be learned").

2. **Pray for wisdom to understand the meaning of the Proverbs and their application to your life.**

---

[1] I'm indebted to Larry Coy who developed the basic outline of the material in this Appendix and to Jim Logan who first taught it to me.

"But if any of you lacks wisdom, let him ask of God, Who gives to all men generously and without reproach, and it will be given to him" (James 1:5).

3.   Choose an appropriate chapter (or topical study).

The book of Proverbs contains 31 chapters. There are 31 days in most months of the year. Many people prefer to divide the book into daily sections, studying the chapter corresponding to the day of the month.[1] Another option is to read portions from a topically arranged Book of Proverbs[2] (or a computer generated facsimile).

4.   Read the entire chapter (slowly), noting (recording) any verses that have special interest to you.

Based on the initial concerns, questions, and issues you began with in step one, certain verses may prove more relevant than others.[3] Make note of these.

5.   Reread all the verses you have written down and select one verse that especially stands out.

The purpose of this project is to become familiar with and to internalize one Proverb during each study session. From the verses that you found especially interesting, select one you would most like to understand and apply to your life.

6.   Interpret (discover and record the meaning of) the verse.

You may want to paraphrase the verse as accurately as possible in your own words. Of course, this will require the use of some study helps such as a variety of Bible translations, lexicons, and commentaries (Bridges, Phillips, Adams, and Arnot).

---

[1] Chapters 1, 2, and 31 of Proverbs are a bit difficult to do using this format since not many of the verses can be understood independently from the others. The same is true elsewhere in Proverbs where several verses are grouped together and do not stand alone, as do the majority of verses in this Book. When interpreting and applying such verses, be sure to do so in the context of those relevant passages on either side of them.

[2] See *Wisdom for Today's Issues: A Topical Arrangement of The Proverbs* by Stephen Voorwinde (Phillipsburg, NJ: Presbyterian and Reformed Publishing).

[3] Of course, the verses may not have any relevance to your initial question or current milieu. In such cases choose verses of interest based on other criteria applicable to you or someone you know.

7. Identify at least two key words (or concepts that are not necessarily in the text) which will help you remember the verse.
The idea behind this step is to find a couple of words that will help you relate the passage to specific issues in life. Sometimes words that do not appear in the text may help you remember the verse more easily. (Example: for Proverbs 14:4, "Where no oxen are, the manger is clean; But much increase [comes] by the strength of the ox," you might use the phrase, "No pain—no gain.") Hopefully, when facing an appropriate set of circumstances (milieu) in the future, you will more easily recall the passage which you have filed away in your heart under these key words.

8. Memorize the entire verse.
At this point, committing the passage to memory should be easy since you've already read the passage several times, interpreted it, and identified two of its key words. Memorize the verse (word for word, tense for tense) in the version of your choosing.

9. See how many life applications of that verse you can make in 5-10 minutes.
Ask, "in how many ways is this verse applicable to my milieu? (At home? At work? At play? At school? In church?) Might this passage apply to the milieu of others I know or have known? How might I apply this passage to a set of circumstances I may encounter in the future?"

> *Warning:* Care should be taken at this point not to overlook other relevant portions of Scripture that may balance, expand or limit the application of the verse you have chosen. Developing a systematic theology (the systematizing of everything the Bible has to say about a particular subject into one balanced and sound doctrinal position) is one of the best ways to avoid foolish decisions and theological errors.

10. Make one personal application of the verse which you can put into practice today (or tomorrow).
Is there a particular sin I've been convicted of which I should confess to God? Is there some attitude, action, thought pattern, or motive that I must, by God's grace, replace with its biblical alternative? Is there a

biblical principle I should put into practice today? Is there a project I can design that will help me implement a truth into my life over the next few weeks?

> *Note:* For younger children (ages 7-10) this study can be simplified by having the child(ren) pick out a verse for discussion as the parent reads an appropriate section of verses, explains, and applies the passage in the milieu to the child(ren)'s life.

The Fallacy of Humanism[1]

The material in this appendix originally appeared in several Christian periodicals. I've included it so that you may help your children more clearly identify humanistic philosophies through a basic knowledge and proper understanding of Scriptural truths.

A. Humanistic Deception

The statements in this column are paraphrases of the points presented in the Humanist Manifesto I (1933). It is prudent when dealing with any philosophy to examine *only the statements* of that philosophy in light of Scripture. It is dangerous to study the reasoning and logic which support that philosophy, since it is possible to think logically to an unbiblical and hence wrong conclusion (Romans 16:19).

Remember, a deception does not necessarily have to be an outright lie. In fact, often the most deceptive statements contain a large amount of truth. Furthermore, even the truth can be stated in such a way as to insinuate things that are not true. This may be one reason why so many have bought the bill of goods peddled by the devil and his Humanistic henchmen.

B. Biblical Truth

Although only one Biblical argument is usually presented in each section, various Scriptural truths may be found that will refute many of the deceptions listed in this chart.

C. Related Scripture

Reviewing these Scriptures should cause the Christian to see the subtle lies of humanism more clearly. The list, however, is not intended to be exhaustive, and you are encouraged to expand these references through personal study.

---

[1] Revised from an article written by the author and first printed in the *Calvary Review*, Spring, 1980. © Calvary Bible College. All Rights Reserved.

Humanistic Deception	Biblical Truth	Scripture
1. Our universe came into existence apart from divine intervention.	Our universe was designed and created by the living God.	Gen. 1 Ps. 136:5-9 Heb. 11:3 2 Pet. 3:3-7
2. The human race evolved from lower forms of life over a very long period of time.	God created man as a complete creature at one point in time.	Gen. 1:27, 28 1 Cor. 15:39 1 Cor. 15:45 2 Pet. 3:3, 4
3. Man is basically an animal, and as such, has no spirit or spiritual capacity—his mind is not distinct from his body.	Man was made in the image of God; he has a mind, a spirit, and a spiritual capacity for the things of God.	John 3:6 1 Cor. 2:11 2 Cor. 4:16 1 Thess. 5:23
4. To satisfy certain social, environmental, and emotional needs, man has created his own religions and passed them on to succeeding generations.	Not all religion is man-made. Christianity is not man trying to reach God, but rather God initiating a program to redeem and restore Adam's fallen race.	John 3:16, 17 Rom. 5:8 2 Cor. 5:18, 19 Gal. 4:4, 5
5. To determine the existence and value of any reality, one must rely entirely upon that which can be scientifically proven.	Since God's ways are "higher" than man's ways, man cannot rely solely on the limited knowledge of science to answer questions, but must turn to the infallible Word of God.	Is. 55:9 1 Cor. 1:17-31 1 Cor. 2:12-16 1 Tim. 6:20

Humanistic Deception	Biblical Truth	Scripture
6. There is no longer a need for (the educated) man to believe in the existence of God.	The wicked through the pride of his countenance *will not* seek after God: All his thoughts are "There is no God."	Ps. 10:4, 14:1 Rom. 1:18-23 1 John 2:22
7. Religion consists of that which is capable of intellectually satisfying man (i.e. art, science, labor, philosophy, love, friendship, and recreation).	The Christian is to "set his affection on things above" knowing that the things of this world cannot truly satisfy.	Prov. 27:20 2 Cor. 4:18 Col. 3:1, 2 1 John 2:15-17
8. There are no eternal consequences for sin. "Eat, drink, and be merry, for tomorrow we die."	There are both temporal and eternal consequences for sin.	Luke 12:19-21 Rom. 6:23 Gal. 6:7, 8 Heb. 9:27
9. Man's religious emotions should be refocused from the traditional attitudes of prayer and worship to the humanistic ideals of self-improvement and social well-being.	The most effective means of "self-improvement" and social well-being is the power of the Holy Spirit. Therefore, prayer and worship serve to enhance "self-improvement" and social well-being.	Prov. 14:34 John 4:24 Rom. 8:1-14 Gal. 5:19-23

Humanistic Deception	Biblical Truth	Scripture
10. Religious emotions and attitudes should not be "associated with belief in the supernatural."	Without faith in the supernatural things of God, it is impossible to please Him. For he that comes to God must believe that God lives and that He is worthy of seeking after.	Matt. 22:23-33 Mark 12:30 1 Tim. 6:20 Heb. 11:6
11. As knowledge and education increase, man will be able to solve an increasing number of the world's problems.	Lasting solutions to the problems of life come by living in harmony with the Word of God. "The fear of the Lord is the beginning of knowledge."	Prov. 1:7 Luke 11:28 1 Cor. 1:18-20 2 Pet. 1:5
12. The aim of religion is to strive for personal fulfillment and satisfaction in life.	The aim of the Christian is the Glory of God.	1 Cor. 1:27-31 1 Cor. 6:19-20; 10:31 2 Tim. 2:4
13. The purpose of all institutions and associations (including religious ones) is to satisfy man.	An institution or association (including religious) by itself cannot truly satisfy man. Only God can. (He may use His church to meet certain needs, but ultimately, it is only God who satisfies.)	Ps. 103:5 Phil. 4:19 Heb. 13:5 James 1:16, 17

Humanistic Deception	Biblical Truth	Scripture
14. A capitalistic society is unfair to the poor; therefore, a society guaranteeing equal rights should be established.	Although Christians are to protect the rights of others, God does not promise everyone equal rights in this life.	Prov. 29:13, 14 Is. 14:12-14 Phil. 4:11-13 1 Tim. 6:1-8
15. Humanism will ultimately result in a satisfactory life for all.	Because man's heart is deceitful above all things and desperately wicked, and because of the existence of a personal devil, it is impossible for man to achieve any form of peaceful universal society apart from Christ.	Jer. 17:9 Matt. 10:34-39 2 Tim. 3:1-7 Rev. 20:1-3

appendix e

A Word to Wives

Let's face it, ladies! The chances are, you will be the one using the resources in this book more than your husbands will. I say this, not because I'm supposing your husbands will be dilatory in the fulfillment of their child rearing responsibilities (although I know very well how few Christian men take God's direct commands to them in Deuteronomy 6 and Ephesians 6 seriously), but because of the simple fact that you will almost certainly be spending more time one-on-one with the children than will your masculine counterparts.

After reading this book you may be motivated to immediately begin putting into practice what you have learned—whether or not your husband is on the same page with you. Please remember, God has given him the responsibility to be the manager of your home; you, therefore, must be careful not to prematurely take these matters into your own hands. Ideally, it would be most beneficial if you and your husband could read this book together, chapter by chapter, applying its various truths to each of your children. However, if for some reason you do not have your husband's interest or cooperation, there is much in this book you can begin to do on your own. Hopefully, in time, your husband will see the positive impact the Bible is having on your children and will inquire where you learned to do what you are doing. But you may not be able to do everything you've learned as effectively without his participation as you could if he were an active participant.

Of particular concern is the matter of having formal family devotions (what I have referred to in this book as "family time"). Very often wives will expect their husbands to lead family worship on a daily or almost daily basis. This expectation, when unfulfilled, can lead to sinful anger, bitterness, or resentment if you allow it to. And it can even tempt a woman to begin to start doubting her husband's spiritual leadership. Guard your heart against any "letter of the law" legalism which thinks, "If my husband doesn't conduct a formal family worship time every single day, he is not doing his job." Remember, the command to fathers in Deuteronomy 6 is *not* to conduct four separate formal "family devotions" each and every day, but rather to teach the Scriptures to their children whenever and wherever life takes them.

Certainly, one significant way a father can pass along his faith in Christ is through a family devotional time. Historically, Jewish, church, and Puritan fathers put a great amount of emphasis on teaching their children. I can't recall meeting many professing Christian women who did not desire their husbands to lead the family in regular Bible reading and prayer times. It's a good desire. A Christian wife who is married to a professing Christian husband should certainly have the freedom to ask her husband to minister to the family by providing structured times of family worship.

But how should a wife respond if her Christian husband is not willing to make a regular commitment to family devotions or communicates a willingness but does not follow through? Here are some suggestions:

- She can make a well thought out and respectful appeal to him.
- She can pray that God will give her husband the desire to lead family devotions and the grace to be consistent.
- A wife can do a lot to make family worship more of a joy and less of a burden to her husband.
- She can remind him of the days and times which were agreed on for the meeting.
- She can be sure that the place where the devotional is to be held is prepared and tidy.
- She can keep him apprised of the individual character flaws of each child and suggest passages to study as a family.
- She can ask her husband if she may remind him verbally or in more subtle ways. I once heard of a wife who, with permission, helped her husband by placing a devotional book beside his dinner plate.
- Instead of expecting daily family times, the wife may suggest that they begin by meeting formally or "officially" only once or twice each week. Be patient and remember that it takes time to establish a habit.

- She can offer to lead the devotional herself when the husband is not at home and, with his permission, encourage the older children to occasionally take turns facilitating "family time."
- She should also be sensitive to her husband's many other daily responsibilities. A godly helper does not contentiously nag her husband—especially about occasional lapses in his daily routine.

If your husband is not involved with regular Bible reading and prayer with the children, you will have to assume this responsibility. When married to an unbelieving or otherwise uninterested spouse, it may be better to do this at a time when the father is not at home in order to not accentuate any lack of interest in spiritual things on his part and to provide him more time with the children while he is at home.

Here are some other suggestions to help make family time more of a consistent reality in your home.
- Keep in mind that since each family is unique and there is no "right" way to have family devotions, the frequency and structure will be different for every family.
- Use mealtime as a natural time to have "family time." (Many households find the time immediately following the evening meal to be best suited for family time.)
- Be creative. Variety is the spice of life when it comes to Bible study and "family time."
- Consider the ages of the children. Families with several young children will find it more difficult to establish a "family time."
- Don't be discouraged. Kids grow up! Additionally, fathers are more likely to be involved with structured Bible times with their children as they mature.
- Be flexible. Don't be legalistic. Allow for changes in the family, schedule, or needs of the children.

Be careful not to get so discouraged with your husband's mishandling of family devotions that it becomes a source of bitterness in your own heart and a point of contention in your marriage. Don't elevate your own desire for your husband to initiate family devotions above the commands of Scripture. Don't turn this good desire into an idolatrous one! A man's commitment to lead "formal family devotions" is not necessarily a barometer of his spiritual maturity or his desire to lead the family spiritually. Guard your heart against comparing your husband or your family to anyone else. An older woman I know once said, "I count it a blessing to have had a husband who lived devotionally rather than having one who only led devotions."

appendix f
Selective Bibliography of Helpful Resources

English Bible Concordance

New Strong's Exhaustive Concordance of the Bible, by James
Strong. Kansas City, MO: Thomas Nelson, 1990.
Treasury of Scripture Knowledge, edited by Jerome H. Smith.
Nashville, TN: Thomas Nelson, 1992.

Topical Bible

Nave's Topical Bible, edited by Orville Nave. Nashville, TN: Thomas Nelson, 1997.

Computer Bibles

Logos Bible Software v. 2.0. Oak Harbor, WA: Logos Research
Systems Inc., 1996.

Bible Dictionaries and Concordances

Theological Dictionary of the New Testament, by Gerhard Kittel et
al. Grand Rapids, MI: Eerdmans, 1986.
Theological Wordbook of the Old Testament, edited by Richard
Harris. Chicago, IL: Moody Press, 1980.
Vine's Expository Dictionary of Biblical Words, by W.E. Vine and
M.F. Unger. Nashville, TN: Thomas Nelson, 1985.

Bible Commentaries

Calvin's Commentaries: 22 Volume Set. Grand Rapids, MI: Baker,
1996.
Commentary on the Whole Bible, by Matthew Henry. Peabody,
MA: Hendrickson Publishers, 1997.

The Expositor's Bible Commentary, edited by Frank E. Gaebelein. Grand Rapids, MI: Zondervan, 1992.

Miscellaneous Bible Study Tools

Biblical Interpretation: The Only Right Way, by D. Kuske. Milwaukee, WI: Northwestern Publishing House, 1995.

How to Read the Bible for All its Worth (2nd ed.), by G. D. Fee & D. Stuart. Grand Rapids, MI: Zondervan, 1993.

International Standard Bible Encyclopedia, edited by G. W. Bromiley. Grand Rapids, MI: Eerdmans, 1995.

Manners and Customs of Bible Lands, by Fred Wright. Chicago, IL: Moody Press, 1953.

Methodical Bible Study, by A. Traina. Grand Rapids, MI: Zondervan Publishing House, 1980.

The Christian Counselor's New Testament, by Jay E. Adams. Woodruff, SC: TIMELESS TEXTS, 1977, 1980, 1994.

The Sufficiency of Scripture, by N. Weeks. Carlisle, PA: The Banner of Truth Trust, 1988.

Thy Word is Truth, by J. Young. Grand Rapids, MI: Eerdmans, 1957.

What to Do on Thursday, by Jay E. Adams. Woodruff, SC: TIMELESS TEXTS, 1982, 1995.

Helpful Puritan Works

A Christian Directory, by Richard Baxter. Morgan, PA: Soli Deo Gloria, 1996.

Of Domestic Duties, by William Gouge. Edmonton AB, Canada: Still Waters Revival Books, 1622 (bound photocopy available).

Other Helpful Bible Study Resources for Child Training

Homework Manual for Biblical Living, by Wayne Mack. 2 vols. Phillipsburg, NJ: Presbyterian and Reformed, 1991.

Quick Scripture Reference for Counseling, by John G. Kruis. Grand Rapids, MI: Baker, 1988.

Ripening Sonship: A Wise Father's Counsel to His Son, by Ron Allchin. Cudahy, WI: Reminder Printing, 1994.

Other Helpful Books on Biblical Parenting

Age of Opportunity: A Biblical Guide to Parenting Teens, by Paul David Tripp. Phillipsburg, NJ: Presbyterian and Reformed, 1997.

Christian Living In the Home, by Jay E. Adams. Grand Rapids, MI: Baker Book House, 1972.

For Instruction in Righteousness, by Pam Forster. Gaston, OR: Doorposts, (503) 357-4749, 1993.

The Family Worship Book, by Terry L. Johnson and Ross-Shire. Great Britain: Christian Focus Publications, 1998.

The Heart of Anger, by Lou Priolo. Amityville, NY: Calvary Press, 1997.

Hints on Child Training, by H. Clay Trumbull. Eugene, OR: Great Expectations, 1998.

Shepherding a Child's Heart, by Tedd Tripp. Wapwallopen, PA: Shepherd Press, 1995.

Successful Christian Parenting, by John MacArthur. Nashville, TN: Nelson Word, 1999.

Withhold Not Correction, by Bruce Ray. Phillipsburg, NJ: Presbyterian and Reformed, 1978.

Helpful Sites on the Worldwide Web

Biblical Family Soulcare: `http://www.soulcare.org`
Doorposts: `http://www.Doorposts.net`
The Milieu Online:
`http://www.tobiasdesign.com/milieu`
Sound Word Associates: `http://www.soundword.com`